The Life and Times of the Black Pig

Ronald Turnbull

THE LIFE AND TIMES OF THE BLACK PIG
A biography of Ben Macdui

Drawings by Colin Brash

Millrace

First published in Great Britain in 2007 by
Millrace
2a Leafield Road, Disley
Cheshire SK12 2JF
www.millracebooks.co.uk

ISBN: 978-1-902173-25-2

Typeset in Adobe Garamond Pro.
Printed and bound in the United Kingdom
by T J International Ltd, Padstow, Cornwall PL28 8RW

Dedication

To those in whose company I have enjoyed Ben Macdui and, in particular, to Colin Brash, Professor N Collie, M Grey, Sir P Hepborne, David Howard, T D Lauder, F L Mor, C & D Nethersole-Thompson, Jeff Parr, T Patey, V Regina, H Raeburn, Matt Scase, Simon Trotter, Barbara Turnbull, D G Turnbull, Thomas Turnbull; and in memory of Oliver Turnbull.

Advice to readers

The routes up Ben Macdui included here are intended to be followed, and as often as possible. The author would welcome any corrections or updates sent via the publisher. However, this book does not aim to assess danger or instruct in hill skills. Hillgoers must consult instructional manuals or professional guides, or else, in the spirit of the people in these pages, make their own judgements. Unroped scrambling is risky, as are the acts described in Chapter 8, and the Cairngorm plateau's winter climate is sometimes lethal. With regard to the one specific danger of Ben Macdui (Chapter 16), it is highly advisable, when overnighting at the Shelter Stone, to leave the whisky either in the entrance or under a completely separate stone. In case of overnight snowdrifts, this stone should be clearly marked.

Contents

Introduction

Mountain.
Peaks pierce the green sky, unblunted.
The sky would fall
but for the columns of mountains.

Mao Zedong: 'Draft Decision of the Central Committee
of the Chinese Communist Party on Certain Problems
in Our Present Rural Work'

Every year, 100,000 folk traipse up the Pony Path
on Ben Nevis, eat their sandwiches, and traipse back
down again. Ben Macdui, Britain's second highest
mountain, attracts a rather different clientele. In 1865,
Queen Victoria on her pony (also called Victoria);
in 1930, an Irishman on a bicycle who thought he
was on his way through the Lairig Ghru; in 1942, an
English army officer in his jeep. Two men I met in
Glen Feshie say their finest form of fun is to ride bikes
up the track to the Ptarmigan Restaurant on Cairn
Gorm, carry the machines across the boulders to Ben
Macdui, and then attempt to ride them down Coire
Etchachan. Some even arrive on foot: in particular,
the non-existent yeti-type monster Ferlas Mor who
treks up from the Garbh Uisge whenever the mist

1

comes down, to gnaw the abandoned sandwiches around the cairn.

Once shaped by the Ice Age, Macdui stood for 20,000 years as just some miscellaneous mountain until its patron the Duke of Fife planned himself a tomb on top, to raise his hill to the level of being the UK's outstanding mountain. Fife died before he could get his gravestone erected (there's a lesson here for all of us) and Macdui retired into life as 'just another hill'.

And yet, in the high-point obsessed culture of today, Macdui continues to stand for certain values at once old-fashioned and curiously modern. Quietly, slightly out of the public eye, Macdui has been preserving the fundamental mountain mysteries. The approach not from the high car-park but under the ancient pines; the wholesome discipline of the Long Walk In. Routefinding up crags of rounded granite, with few firm belay points, but an abundance of plant-life and slime. The two hours uphill on stones. The noble art of axe and crampons, the occasional killer blizzard, and the fun of not falling through a cornice in a white-out. The poem in the Gaelic. The flat, flat summit and the gently rounded summit view.

Ben Macdui is a 500-million year-old lump of magma exposed by erosion and half chewed away by a glacier. But this book is not so much about the summit, as the stories we tell ourselves on the way up there. Some of them are fairy stories, and some are the more serious bits of fiction we call history. Some are the peculiarly plausible stories called science.

But the most important stories are about the heroes of hillwalking, the pointless adventure on the Forefinger Pinnacle. These are the tales we tell ourselves to make it all make sense. As you stand below the avalanche, battle the stormy plateau, or cross thawing ice of Loch Avon, these stories are not just serious but deadly serious. In the twenty-first century, self-deception is one of the survival arts. Lose the plot, and end up in front of the TV with a premature heart attack.

A walk is a story, and any story is in some sense a walk. The way to make friends with a lump of eroded granite is with the feet. The various fictional and literary expeditions here are arranged geographically, north to south, starting at Glen More and the Pass of Ryvoan.

But now it's time for the book's hero. That is, if you're really sure you want to meet Mr Macdui? He lives, it has to be said, in rather low company. In under the Shelter Stone are lurking robbers and fugitives, whisky-smugglers and deer-poachers, tinkers and three dancing tailors, caterans and caitiffs and Queen Victoria in disguise. Here in their stinking breeches are mountain men of the twentieth century and, more especially, those of the breed from Aberdeen.

But it's sleeting outside, so come in under. That bearded man asleep and snoring with his boots on—ignore him, he's been there since 1789. Shove aside some sodden rucksacks and make yourself at home among the mouse-droppings and torn plastic sheeting. Two thousand tons of cold grey granite are above you, and two centuries of food remnants and historic litter are slowly decomposing under your bum. The breeze flaps the plastic, a few snowflakes drift through the light of the candle. There's a long night ahead.

Notes

For the serious scholar, some notes on sources are at chapter ends.

SMCJ = Scottish Mountaineering Club Journal

CCJ = Cairngorm Club Journal

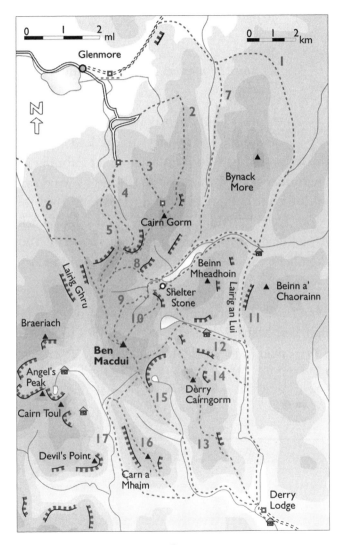

Glenmore

0 1 2 ml

0 1 2 km

N

7

1

2

3

4

Bynack More

Cairn Gorm

5

6

Laing Ghru

8

Beinn Mheadhoin

9

Shelter Stone

10

Lairig an Lui

Beinn a' Chaorainn

11

Braeriach

Ben Macdui

12

Angel's Peak

Cairn Toul

14

Derry Cairngorm

15

17

16

13

Devil's Point

Carn a' Mhaim

Derry Lodge

ROUTE 1 *Loch Avon and the Shelter Stone*

Start:	Glenmore village
Distance to summit:	24km (15 miles)
Total ascent:	1,200m (4,000ft)

Heron's Field car-park doesn't have any pay-and-display machines. Tracks lead through the forest and past Lochan Uaine to a footbridge at the former site of Bynack Stable (shelter blown down in 2005 and removed). Well-used path to Fords of Avon. Head upstream, then along west side of Loch Avon (or less-pathed east side if river crossable) to the Shelter Stone. Eroded path passes foot of Loch Etchachan onto Macdui.

How good? The long, interesting and imposing route that Ben Macdui deserves. The night at the Shelter Stone could be avoided but shouldn't be.

1 Avon and Etchachan

And see not ye that braid braid road
That lies across yon lilly leven?
That is the path of wickedness
Tho' some call it the road to heaven…

Thomas Rhymer, on not taking the
standard route from the car-park

The braid braid road to Ben Macdui is actually rather
low on lilies. It substitutes a number of granite stones,
and quite a lot of moss, as it wends its way up the
Fiacaill Ridge of Coire Cas, around the corrie's head
wall, and then across the plateau among the grey
hillocks to the cairn. And then back again.

The Rule of Hillwalking says: walk up the hills.
And we must accept that rule without question, for
questioning risks us ending up in front of the TV
watching the cricket.

Having unquestioningly accepted the necessity
of Ben Macdui, it makes sense to get there from the
north. That route is much shorter than any line from
Linn of Dee, and the top car-park is already half-way
up the hill.

But who says hillwalking has to make sense?

Getting it done quick and easy is great if you're in a hurry to start watching the cricket. But given that the hill is supposed to be a substitute for the sofa, it makes even more sense to do it as slowly as possible. The standard route from the car-park, as celebrated by all the guidebook writers: yes it's good, and (as in Chapter 4), even better in bad weather. But take two days to do Ben Macdui, and have twice as much fun. (And don't worry—the cricket will still be grinding on towards its inevitable draw.)

So park at Heron's Field and take the track by the riverside with the broom bushes. Turn left away from the water and walk into the forest: the tall red trunks of the pines, and the heather hummocks, and the sandy path winding between. Every summit walk should start off under the trees, and then out beside the green lochan, where the fairies rinse out their smalls between high slopes of grey-blue scree and red-brown heather. Overhead, a few pines strike attitudes described in an account of 1875 as 'daring and picturesque'.

Emerge from the pass, and you're at the end of the Thieves' Road out of Lochaber. And confronted with the thief's choice: to raid northwards down the Nethy, forwards into Aberdeen, or to turn south through the Lairig, for the Glens of Angus? So many cows, so short a life for stealing them... But since what we're actually after is no cow but the Hill of the Black Pig, we take the right-hand fork for Bynack Stable.

The sandy track crosses moorland, with bright lochans among the brown, and single pine trees here and there, ready to link branches between Glen More and the Abernethy. And maybe, in the very century that's now started, the first squirrel shall run twig to twig from Grantown to Dalwhinnie.

The track ends at a footbridge and a patch of ground where Bynack Stable used to stand. The stable, always a chilly open-sided shelter, blew down in 2005. The RSPB, which owned it, tidily took away the pieces. The ground where it stood is bright green, many walkers having poured out their liquid nitrates against or, squalid fellows, within its former walls.

The old drove path climbs across the flank of Bynack More and into a slightly sheltered hollow. This is a good place to not get lost. Downvalley, the Water of Caiplich runs north-east for eleven miles, joins the Avon and finally emerges at Tomintoul (which has a bus service back to Aviemore via the Cromarty Firth, a six-hour trip if the connections work out). On either side, low hills are deeply heathered and featureless. If fresh snow covers the path, you'd better be confident in your compass.

The path, supposing it's snowless and you can see it, crosses a hill shoulder and then a pass, and descends a shallow valley, to arrive at the bank of a sudden and surprising large river. The drove path continues ahead through a ford. Just in case the river should be too high for crossing, there's a handy small shelter. It's a metal box, resembling the back-end of a refrigerated container lorry. The roof is low, the floor is decomposing heather, the door clangs shut on total darkness as there is no window.

On a stormy, snowy February morning, I'd been assigned to leave my Glenmore youth hostel bunk at 5.00am to slog through the snow and check out this shelter in case a missing walker had decided to die inside it. But the walker was discovered, still alive, when the pubs closed (and so we got to lie in until 7.30 and slogged through the snow up Cairn Gorm instead).

There's no need on this current walk to take shelter in the Fords of Avon shelter while waiting for the water to go down so's to ford the Fords of Avon. Instead, turn upstream on a rough peaty path for two miles, to clamber over a low mound of granite gravel. And your feet are at the foot of Loch Avon.

Narrow grey water stretches ahead into the heart of the mountains. Up on the right, the ground rises steeply for 1,000 feet to the Stag Rocks, with the summit of Cairn Gorm out of sight above. Up on the left, the ground rises steeply for just under 1,000 feet to the Stacan Dubha, the Black Stacks of Beinn Mheadhoin. As you've had a fairly tough time getting here, I'd ease things a bit and call that last hill Ben Vane. Ben Vane is how you say it, is how you spell it when the same name occurs down beside Loch Lomond, and after all, Gaelic has not been spoken here for a century or so. But Mheadhoin it remains on the map. The name means 'Middle Mountain', and Mheadhoin is indeed a long, long way from anywhere. But you can bag it tonight, if you like, or first thing in the morning.

Stag Rocks on one side, Stacan on the other; but, at the water's head, there's the great square-topped Sticil, or Shelter Stone Crag. Climbers say it's rich in interesting plant life, but from here at the lake foot it's a rectangular block of blank, bare granite. On its left, there's a narrow gap leading out, not to comfort and Braemar, but to Loch Etchachan, the stretch of water that's even higher and bleaker than Loch Avon. And on its right, the ground rises in granite slab and waterfall to the hollows below Ben Macdui.

In front of all of this, as foreground relief, there's a large, rounded granite rock. The rock is coloured, somewhat surprisingly and utterly inappropriately, pale pink.

On a May morning I stood here, leaning into the wind. The slopes ran up from the water to a sprinkling of fresh snow and black wet crags, and then into cloud. A squall brought white horses of foam down the loch towards me, and a whirlwind of flying spray. I photographed it as it came and, as it arrived, dodged behind the pink granite boulder to keep myself and camera dry.

During the years of the chairlift up Cairn Gorm, the paths around Loch Avon got rather large. And that's a damned shame, as Loch Avon does deserve to be as remote as Nature made it. There are spectacular places in Scotland that are easy to get to: Glen Nevis, Glen Coe, Loch an Eilein, Bealach na Ba in Applecross. It is only right that there should also be special places that ask for effort.

The Cairngorm Funicular Railway has 'No Exit' signs at the funicular top station. This may, or may not, lead to the eventual revival of the ptarmigan, dotterel and snow bunting. One particular form of wildlife, however, always finds a congenial habitat: that lively and never-endangered hairy creature, the bugbear. Gosh, I see one coming right now!

Planning consent for the Funicular Railway was

granted on condition that passengers would not escape onto the open hill, there to trample the lichen, fall over the crags, and accidentally wander down to Loch Avon. Pay your £9, hop aboard the tin truck, and your 'mountain experience' consists of: a view through the slightly steamed up windows (at least until you enter the tunnel), an indoor audio-visual display, and a trip to the balcony to look at clouds from the inside. Oh, also two shops plus a restaurant. The promoters of the funicular argued that the disabled and unfit have the same rights as the rest of us to enjoy the mountain experience. But what the poor old punters are getting hasn't anything to do with the mountain and can barely be considered an experience.

I don't know if this peculiar policy is enforceable —footsloggers off the hilltop are allowed in, through a special door, to spend their money in the shops. The paths around Loch Avon do now seem smaller and less worn. However, I suspect this is not down to funny rules at the funicular, but just because the great majority of today's walkers stick strictly to the standard route from car-park to Munro summit and back again.

Oho! Do I spot a second bugbear creeping out behind a boulder to join its little furry friend? Let's pass briskly along the loch side in quest of a more interesting form of wildlife, in the slightly rounded shape of Queen Victoria. She arrived here on 28th September 1861 and was most impressed: 'Nothing could be grander and wilder—the rocks are so grand and precipitous, and the snow on Ben Muich Dhui had such a fine effect.' From their carriages at Derry Lodge, they rode on ponyback by way of Fords of Avon, walking occasionally where the ground was particularly wet or rough, 'rougher than anything we ever rode upon before'; the ghillies, of course, walked it all.

Just past the loch head lies a jumble of great boulders cracked off the Sticil crag. It seems that the rocks fell just after the Ice Age, to slide down deep snowfields below the crag, for the largest of them has alighted gently onto smaller boulders, as if lowered there by melting snow. Thus it forms a cavity or cave. Clach Dhian translates to the Shelter Stone, capable of holding seventeen armed men—or about five fully-equipped hillwalkers of today.

Here, at the head of its wildest stretch of water, below its most formidable crag, and five hours at least from any car-park, is the true heart of the Cairngorms. No hillwalking lifetime is complete without a night spent under this 2,000-ton lump of chilly grey granite. If you need to check in, the Visitors' Book is usually found in the horizontal crack to the right of the entrance.

Enter half-crouching, and stand for a few minutes

Shelter Stone Crag and the Shelter Stone

to let eyes adjust before putting your rucksack or any part of your person on the dirt floor, as there may be something nastier than plain dirt down there.

The seventeen armed men departed some time before the turn of the nineteenth century, leaving space for the painter and watercolourist George Fennel Robson. He arrives dressed in tartan plaid and hose, with the complete *Waverley Novels* of Sir Walter Scott behind him on his pony. Robson drew Ben Macdui but didn't get to the top, though he achieved Braeriach. He describes the Falls of Tarf, in Glen Tilt: 'a scene worthy of the pencil of Salvator… nowhere… will be found to possess a more picturesque combination of wild and characteristic beauty than this'; and these phrases, lifted straight out of William Gilpin's *Guide to the Sublime*, reveal him as a well-trained landscape appreciator of the English Lake District tendency.

James Hogg, the poet and friend of Walter Scott known as the Ettrick Shepherd, passed this way around 1802. He considered Loch Avon to be at least six miles long. Has the scenery indeed shrunk? *The Wolfe of Badenoch*, the novel of 1827 by Sir Thomas Dick Lauder, has an accurate description of the Stone itself and the streams at the head of the loch, but in those exciting days Ben Macdui was infested with wolves and wild bison, and had a dangerous glacier blocking the top of Coire Sputan Dearg. The bold Sir Patrick Hepborne plus page Maurice de Grey survive the bison and cross the glacier, to reach the Shelter Stone in Chapter XXVI—and they will do so again in Chapter 7 below. Once there, their sleep was twice disturbed by knife-wielding Gaels, but they woke, like many of us since, to a pale and lovely sunrise.

Walter A Smith and party, real non-fictional people visiting in 1875, also suffered Gaelic-speaking intruders in the middle of the night; they took them to be poachers after a trout or two out of Loch Avon. The boy W Inglis Clarke (father, as it were, of the Charles Inglis Clarke Hut on Ben Nevis) also shared the stone with unsavoury locals who arrived in the dark. The two schoolboys had attempted to light a fire and their damp smoke drove off the night visitors who retreated with 'strange oaths'. The fire having failed them, the boys resorted to re-climbing Ben Macdui, through fresh snow, simply to warm up.

Two of the first specifically hillwalking victims of the Cairngorms, Alistair Mackenzie and Duncan Ferrier, spent the first night of 1933 and the last of their lives under the Shelter Stone. Their bodies were found eight days later on the Glenmore slope of Cairn Gorm. Here, too, have been at least two sightings of the mysterious Grey Man of Macdui. And all the biggest and ugliest Aberdeen hardmen have stamped their naily boots into this dirty floor. Midges tend not to come into the chilly shades underneath the big stone, but there is at least one mouse.

Human intruders may, however, be fewer than in the 1820s. Odd, as today's advances in plaid technology mean that you can at least lie in a comfortable down-filled bag as you shiver through the night. At last dawn's grey light seeps around the socks hopefully drying on a string across the entrance tunnel. In theory, the 2,000 tons of granite overhead should hold the day's warmth through into the night. That doesn't seem to happen, but it's a lot better at holding the night's chill through into the morning. It's not going to get any nicer, so you might as well get up right now. In August, the sunrise aligns itself perfectly along Loch Avon. And under the rock, you can't really tell the weather: there might be a pale and lovely sunrise out there.

Starting from the Stone, and once you've shivered the chill out of your bones, there's an inspiring choice of ways upwards. Castlegates and Pinnacle Gullies are grim but scenic. The Avon Slabs are the best sort of scramble, always on rock but with the amount of easiness entirely up to yourself. The natural line, though, is by the steep path under the Sticil buttress and up to Loch Etchachan.

Loch Avon that you just left is larger than any

other body of water in the UK of the same altitude. If you're a body of water and you're higher than Loch Avon then you're also smaller than Loch Avon. Loch Etchachan *is* higher than Loch Avon, and accordingly is smaller than Loch Avon; however, among all the bodies of water higher (and smaller) than Loch Avon, it's the biggest. Accordingly, Loch Etchachan, also, is larger than any other body of its same altitude or higher. (And the same again is true of little Lochan Buidhe, at 1,040 metres on the Macdui plateau.)

Loch Avon is romantically bleak: Loch Etchachan is just bleak. Stones surround it, enlivened by a patch of bright mossy bog at its foot. Here are no inspiring crags, but low-angled damp slabs and slopes of old snow. Although it's a loch, it lies at a height properly belonging to a hilltop. And, like a hilltop, it has views. As you arrive, look back north along the grandeur of Loch Avon. As you reach the outflow, the eye slides eastwards down Coire Etchachan to the Lairig an Lui and Beinn a' Bhuird. And a short stony climb ahead brings you to the edge overlooking Coire Sputan Dearg; here you see southwards towards the Derry and the Dee.

The wide, well-used path leads up though scenery ever bleaker. Bare stones and gravel lead to the plateau, where you'll be surprised by the quite large

Tailors' Burn running across your path. Even more surprising are the pink cushions of moss campion here in early summer. The snow bunting, too, is up here somewhere, a flicker of bright black-and-white among the grey. Plus, if it's chilly-clear, you see half the hills of Scotland. In theory, Ben Hope on the north coast is in sight; an easier eye-line is the notable cone of Morven in Sutherland, due north across the Beauly Firth and 81 miles away. In the south, you can even see England: Cheviot, 125 miles away, should be directly above Carn a' Gheoidh, supposing you can work out which one is Carn a' Gheoidh (a very minor Munro south of Braemar). Easier to spot is West Lomond in Fife, roughly south; a vague shadow beyond it is the Moorfoots the other side of Edinburgh.

The computer confirms, what was long a topic of speculation in the Scottish Mountaineering Club Journal, that no part of the Cuillin is visible from here. That's a relief—it was hard enough pretending we could see the Cheviot.

When wet fresh snow covers its ankle-twisting boulders, the Macdui plateau is an uncomfortable place. And in a blizzard it can be lethal: there are plenty of crag tops and avalanche slopes to catch you right out in a white-out. But on a summer's day, when the heat strikes back off the boulders but the air is cool and clear, it's a very pleasant place indeed. Gravel bits between the boulders are easy underfoot. A low ruin waymarks the final quarter-mile: it's the Sappers' Hut, built by the surveyors who lived up here through the summer of 1847 as they worked out the shape of Scotland. Those surveyors confirmed finally that Macdui was 112 feet lower than Ben Nevis, though that fact had been known for forty years to all but Deeside die-hards.

Another couple of hundred yards, and you're at the cairn. The concrete trig point is on top of it, which presumably means it doesn't count and Macdui is actually six feet lower even than supposed. A nearby topograph lets you look at the views (or at least an anodised version) in any cloud cover with more than a metre of visibility.

In that mist, this is a mysterious other-worldly place, and jolly difficult to find your way down off. In real wind, it can be dangerous even to climb down off the cairn and back onto the boulders. January coats it in hoar-frost, patterned all over like a frigid sort of seaweed wafting in an ocean of snowflakes. In high summer, you might just meet the Glenmore reindeer herd. At dawn, there could be the Brocken spectre; at night, it's almost certainly the Great Grey Man.

Summer and winter, darkness and dawn: it's a spot you'll be coming back to several times again.

Notes and references

(p7) The ballad 'Thomas Rhymer' appears in Volume I of *The English and Scottish Popular Ballads*, edited by Francis James Child; and on the Internet.

(p16) Robson: Ian Mitchell, *Scotland's Mountains before the Mountaineers*, Chapter 2.

(p16) Dick Lauder: see Chapter 7.

(p17) Smith: SMCJ 3 (Sept 1890), XIV (1917) and 22 (1940).

(p17) Inglis Clark: SMCJ XVI (1922).

(p17) Accident of 1933: SMCJ 20 (1935).

(p20) Computer view from Macdui:
www.viewfinderpanoramas.org

ROUTE 2 *North Ridge of Cairn Gorm*

Start: Coire na Ciste car-park
Distance to summit: 13km (8 miles)
Total ascent: 1,050m (3,500ft)

Contour east; a path turns briefly down-stream beside Allt na Ciste, then dips to cross Allt Ban. Cross outflow of Lochan na Beinne, and head up to left of a felled plantation onto the ridge. Follow it over Cnap Coire na Spreidhe to Cairn Gorm—the small path is intermittent, and needs some care in cloud.

Head down west, to skirt the head of Coire an t-Sneachda to the cairn below Cairn Lochan (NH992027). Path contours south to Lochan Buidhe (which may be frozen and invisible under snow) then skirts west of North Top to the summit. North Top has only small cairns, the true summit has a large one with trig point on top.

How good? An enjoyable ridge, less busy and much more beautiful than the ways up through the ski area.

2 Enough, Macduff?

Lay on, Macduff; and curs'd be he that first cries hold, enough!

Shakespeare: *Macbeth,* Act V

Ben Macdui may not be 'Binn-na-Muick-duidh', the Hill of the Black Pig, at all. Another version has it as Macduff's Hill. And on Pont's map of 1608 it does indeed appear as Ben Macduff. Macduff, we might remember from Shakespeare, was Thane of Fife, his wife and children murdered by Macbeth in Act IV. ('What, all my pretty chickens and their dam, at one fell swoop?') His successors, the Earls of Fife, owned bits of the Cairngorms from the twelfth century, though they didn't get hold of Ben Macdui itself until the eighteenth century. The Earl of Mar, its former owner, lost his big hill for supporting the wrong side in the rebellion of 1715.

The Fifes lived at Mar Lodge on Deeside, greeting their guests in a ballroom containing 2,435 sets of red deer antlers. Thus they were neighbours of Queen Victoria, and the fifth Earl paid court to the queen's granddaughter Princess Alice. 'An excellent match,' the Queen wrote in her diary: 'he is exceedingly rich.'

When the Revd Dr Keith in 1810 revealed that Ben Macdui was only Scotland's second highest mountain, the then Earl conceived the plan of building himself a mausoleum on the summit of Macdui, a structure which at 100 feet would more than make up the 51-foot deficit. (Today's measurements would leave it still three feet too low: bother!) It was to be a massive stone pyramid, rather like the one Victoria raised for her Albert in the woods above Balmoral. Albert's one, despite mature trees, can be seen from a distance of five or six miles, poking above the pine-tops. The Fife Spike was to be roughly twice as high, and was to include a burial chamber, in the manner of the Egyptians.

The poor mad fool. For it is generally agreed among mountain measurers that man-made additions *don't count*. The cairn of 22 feet built in the 1890s on Ben Lawers (3,980 feet) did not raise the mountain itself above the 4,000-foot mark. An even bigger one was required on 2,970-foot Aran Fawddwy to fail to turn it into a Welsh threethousand—for this was a popular sort of lark, getting summits up to some rounded number of feet. Journalists from *Trail* magazine took a fibreglass fake hilltop onto Beinn Dearg Torridon (2,998 feet), claimed it as a Munro, bagged it, and took their top away before anyone else could get it ticked on their list. A bag, yes; but a *plastic* bag.

Man-made subtractions, on the other hand, do count. If Roineval in Harris is eventually turned into roadstone and removed in large barges, it won't be possible to consider it as still being 1,580 feet high. (The superquarry is currently rejected and Roineval remains as a fine small mountain, although, like Macdui/Muich-Duibh, suffering an identity crisis as 'Roineabhal', Norse respelt into Gaelic.)

Accordingly, the way to gain Macdui its rightful place as Scotland's top mountain will be surreptitiously some night to remove the top 105 feet of Ben Nevis. Gone the metal shelter and the memorial cairn so much smaller and scruffier than the one grandly planned by Fife for Ben Macdui. Gone the observatory ruins, the trig pillar and the top pitches of Tower Ridge and Observatory Buttress. Imagine the astonishment of two hundred Nevis-walkers the following lunchtime to find the summit plateau sliced off nicely across the base of McLean's Steep. Worse: the Great Tower, across the airy and terrifying Tower Gap, has just become the summit of Ben Nevis.

Don't worry chaps. It's no longer Nevis you need. What you have to do is pile back into the car, head east to Aviemore, and walk up Ben Macdui.

The Ordnance Survey, when they reached Ben Macdui in 1847, built a cairn of 22 feet; that would have been half-way to being up alongside Ben Nevis, except that by that time Nevis had risen to 4,406 feet. Meanwhile, Binn-na-Muick-duidh became, by further misspelling, Ben Muich Dhui and then Ben Macdhui. Macdhui would be pronounced, if at all, as MacOoey; wherever that H belongs, it isn't after the D but somewhere at the end. It was in about 1950 the mountain shrank to 'Macdui'.

Despite his ambitious plans for defacing it, I prefer the hill to be not about Macduff of Fife, but the black pig. The pig in question will be a wild boar, rampaging through the forest of Mar or else of Rothiemurchus.

Notes

(p25) The SMC area guide *The Cairngorms* (1928) mentions Fife's 'sepulchral pyramid', citing Alexander Laing, *The Caledonian Itinerary* (1819).

(p26) On Harvey's *Ben Nevis* summit enlargement, the Great Tower stands at about 1,280 metres. So a bulldozed Nevis might be the hardest mainland Munro, but only fourth-highest.

ROUTE 3 *Cairn Gorm and the Plateau*

Start: Coire Cas car-park
Distance to summit: 9km (6 miles)
Total ascent: 900m (3,000ft)

Start from the lower car-park, so as not to obstruct the upper one, as this would compel Funicular riders to double their distance and ascent (to 100 metres and 20 metres of up).

Pass left of the bottom station and then left under the railway on a path onto the ridge An t-Aonach. Follow this up to the Ptarmigan (Funicular top station), and take the paved path to Cairn Gorm summit. Cross the plateau as on Route 2.

Other ways onto the plateau are straight up under the ski-lifts (ugh) or the Fiacaill Coire an t-Sneachda ridge immediately west of the ski area.

How good? Convenient and quick; useful for starting a fourthousands circuit, or in descent in bad weather. Otherwise, there are better ways.

3 Giants on the Earth
The fourthousands walk

Some folk'll tak' a heap o' fash
For unco little en' man,
An' meikle time and meikle cash
For nocht ava' they'll spen', man.
Thae chaps had come a hunder' mile
For what was hardly worth their while ;
'Twas a' to pu'
Some gerse that grew
On Ben Muich Dhu,
That ne'er a coo
Would care to pit her moo' till.

Anon, in mockery of the ascent of naturalist Professor Bayley Balfour in 1837. (*fash:* trouble; *meikle:* much; *ava':* at all; *pu':* pull; *gerse:* grass; *moo:* mouth; *till:* to)

Taste your legs, Sir; put them to motion
Shakespeare: Twelfth Night, Act III

Before the dawn of History, there roamed across Scotland a race of semi-legendary beings called the Fingalians. Fingalians were larger than life—quite literally. They leapt across whole mountains, and crossed to the Hebridean islands by pole-vaulting on the shafts of their spears. Often they would overshoot, crash-landing in the Atlantic, their broken bodies then forming the smaller and more westerly islands. All these goings-on were chronicled by their bard Ossian, who lived in an inaccessible cave in the side of Bidean nam Bian.

Drowned in the Minch or otherwise, the Fingalians died out, to be replaced by mere people; and for a couple of millennia the mountaintops lay untrodden under the rain. (Or did they? Macdui's Great Grey Man could just be a surviving midget Fingalian.) But then came another race, this time of human beings with beards, who seem similarly larger than life.

In the late nineteenth century, it became apparent that just seven of Scotland's hills rise above 4,000 feet, with four of them forming a neat cluster around the Lairig Ghru. Did the Victorian members of the Scottish Mountaineering Club, in their big hobnailers, wait for the short nights of summer and attempt the circuit of Cairn Gorm, Macdui, Cairn Toul and Braeriach?

They did not. Cairn Gorm, Macdui, Cairn Toul and Braeriach are only four tops, in a ring of barely 25 miles, with barely more ascent than twice up Ben Nevis. That made a suitable walk, not for a long June day, but for snow-covered winter-time for A W Russell and A Fraser in May 1897. They alighted at

Aviemore off the overnight train from Edinburgh and set out at 4.30am. They overcame the steep headwall of Braeriach's Coire an Lochain by plenty of step-cutting and some fun at the cornice. They continued over Angel's Peak, Cairn Toul, Ben Macdui and Cairn Gorm, returning to Aviemore for the 'useful but most uncomfortable' midnight train and back to 'the ordinary office routine' next morning after their one-day weekend.

As a summer-time outing, the fourthousands were crossed together almost by chance, by five Aberdonians in June 1909, as part of a *proper* hill walk of 28 miles from Loch Builg to Loch Einich, a walk that also included Beinn a' Bhuird and Ben Avon. One of the five was Henry Kellas, who later achieved the least unconvincing of the sightings of the Grey Man of Macdui. In June 1904, a party of three including A F Whyte and Hugh Miller (a grandson of Hugh Miller the geologist) toured the fourthousands, but again the four summits weren't nearly enough. They added a descent to the Shelter Stone by glissading Castlegates Gully a month before its official first ascent, followed by a return to Cairn Gorm for the sunrise. They also took in Carn a' Mhaim, Beinn Bhrotain, Monadh Mor, Devil's Point, and Angel's Peak, returning after 23 hours to Loch Morlich.

The Victorians weren't even the first to link up the fourthousanders. The earliest recorded ascent of Ben Macdui, back on 21st September 1810, just happened to take in Braeriach and Cairn Gorm at the same time. The Revd Dr George Skene Keith was minister at Leith Hall near Huntley in Aberdeenshire. Keith lived during the Scottish Enlightenment and corresponded with George Washington on the topic of unifying weights and measures (so that while he may have been only a century ahead of his time in terms of walking the Cairngorms, we have yet to catch up over gallons and ounces…) As an enlightened Scot, he provided himself a scientific motive for his Munro-bagging in the shape of a large barometer. In the summer of 1810, at the age of 58, he got lost coming off Cairn Toul in low cloud and a gale that made it almost impossible to hold the umbrella over the barometer. For his second venture, he crossed Cairn Toul again, followed by Braeriach, descending to Aviemore where the Duke of Gordon kindly lent the party a compass as well as a local guide. The following day they set off from Aviemore at 5.00am, heading first back up Braeriach, then crossing the Lairig Ghru to Ben Macdui. Here over lunch they deployed the barometer, finding themselves to be 50 feet lower down than Ben Nevis (which Keith's son had just been sent to measure). They continued to Cairn Gorm, took a dram at Huntley's Well, and descended to Glenmore: 'a most delightful day' despite having achieved only three of the fourthousanders.

Some time before Keith, the first *unrecorded* ascent of Macdui, leaving aside any Fingalians and Great Grey Men, was probably by a miner of the Cairngorm gemstones, a rather unattractive brown-coloured form of quartz: this was already a significant industry by 1810.

These long-ago Joes were not exceptional. In those days boots were boots, weighing in at 2¼ pounds

Corrour bothy

33

apiece (2kg the pair) and slid across the granite with sparks and a screeching sound—jackets were made of porous tweed, and breeches rubbed you raw between the legs whenever it rained (unless you sensibly wore the kilt, airy and elegant until it came to an unexpected slide down a snowfield)—maps were often wrong and weather forecasts always were—there was no convenient car-park under Coire Cas and no convenient car to drive up to it either. In that ancient age, these elderly fellows outwalked us by as much as half a dozen hills a day.

Their secret was simply that, the first generation of mountaineers, they were also the last generation that walked all the time in their daily lives. They walked not only farther than their Gore-tex wearing great-grandchildren, but a fair bit faster. Nobody now keeps up Naismith's pace of 3mph (and an hour for every 2,000 feet of climb) up and down the sides of Ben Macdui. Their technique may have involved a particular rotation of the hips to extend each stride —as still used by the small group of sportspeople, the competitive race-walkers.

In the 1920s, serious-minded hikers from Manchester's Rucksack Club started aiming explicitly for faster times and longer distances. In June 1924, Eustace Thomas, Rooke Corbett and three others crossed all Scotland's 4,000-foot tops—Lochaber as well as Cairngorms—in just 22 hours 38 minutes from the roadside below Aonach Mor to Braeriach summit. Their adventures included a bar meal in Fort William at 10.00pm (try getting that today!) and emergency repairs not to the car but to the road itself, using a handy plank, on the way up Glen More.

Today we don't have the good luck to walk six miles and more to school daily from the age of four. This leaves just one way of keeping up with these early walkers: that is, to run.

The first really fast time around the fourthousands was by the fellrunner Eric Beard, who in 1963 took just 4 hours 41 minutes. His circuit started and finished at Cairngorm Lodge youth hostel (which at that time was Glenmore Lodge outdoor training centre) and didn't include Angel's Peak, which had lost its Munro status in 1921. In 2004, running solo and unsupported, Alec Keith reduced this to 4 hours 21 minutes. He took just 21 minutes from Cairn Toul summit to the River Dee, and 14 minutes from Cairn Gorm to the car-park. The fastest woman, some time in the 1980s, was Kath Butler in 6 hours 45 minutes.

The all-Scotland fourthousanders have now been achieved, without the car, by Martin Stone—he took 21 hours 39 minutes in 1986. The seventeen Cairngorm Munros (Angel's Peak again excluded) have been achieved within 24 hours three times, the fastest and most recent circuit being by Phil Clark in 2004. The circuit from Glenmore covers 76 miles with 33,000 feet of ascent (122 kilometres horizontal and 10 kilometres straight up).

So giants do still roam the mountaintops in these days. It's just that they tend to be extremely small and skinny giants who wear shorts and little blue shoes.

Notes and references

(p29) Epigraph: the sinister reason for the unwholesomeness of Macdui's grass is in Chapter 16.

(p30) Russell and Fraser: SMCJ XVIII (1928) p214.

(p31) Kellas, etc: cited as the first known fourthousands crossing in SMC *Cairngorms* Guide (1928); in fact both Russell's party and Whyte's have precedence.

(p31) Whyte, A F: *A Cairngorm Chronicle,* Millrace (2007).

(p32) Keith: *Scotland's Mountains before the Mountaineers* by Ian Mitchell (1998), quoting Keith: *A General View of the Agriculture of Aberdeenshire* (1811).

(p33) Weight of boots: Percy Unna, SMCJ xvi p 50.

(p34) Eustace Thomas: SMCJ (1925).

(p35) Scottish Hill Runners www.shr.uk.com: Long-distance records compiled by Alastair Matthewson.

ROUTE 4 *Goat Track to the Plateau*

Start: Coire Cas car-park
Distance to summit: 8km (5 miles)
Total ascent: 700m (2,400ft)

A wide, rebuilt path contours out right (west) signed for the Northern Corries. It turns uphill (ignore side-paths right) and up to the right of the stream into Coire an t-Sneachda. Cross boulders and pass between small lochans to a stretcher box below crags. (From this point the enterprising can embellish the ascent to the plateau. Slant slightly left into an open gully leading to a steep field of grass and stones. Head up this, with path trace, to its top right corner. Straight above is Pygmy Ridge, Grade 3 scramble, or head right across a gully foot and up broken ground to its right, Grade 1 scrambling.)

From the stretcher box a small path slants up to the right below crags, then zigzags steeply up to the cairn in the col below Cairn Lochan (NH992027). Continue ahead across the plateau as Route 2.

How good? Attractive, interesting and, in summer conditions, only slightly demanding. Can be serious under snow.

4 Misty for Me

I need to embarrass myself—it kills boredom.
How wonderful it is to get lost!

Verlaine

Play Misty for Me: Clint Eastwood's 1971 thriller is an invitation to terror—where the scream you hear may well be your own—as Jessica Walker becomes angry and upset, destroys your possessions, knifes your cleaning lady and kidnaps your girlfriend, while constantly wanting to hear 'Misty', the Erroll Garner classic from 1954 (lyrics by Johnny Burke): 'Never knowing my right foot from my left, my hat from my glove / I'm too misty, and too much in love.'

Johnny Burke, so he says in the song, felt like he was clinging to a cloud. Clint Eastwood ended up in the Bernese Oberland, dangling from the North Face of the Eiger with, to make it all more exciting, Dougal Haston as his safety officer—Haston being perhaps the least sensible of a generation of non-risk-averse Scottish climbers. Me, I was only on my way back from Ben Macdui, taking in Cairn Gorm because the weather station does make such a handy waypoint, and concentrating hard so as not to get my glove on my head and my hands trapped in my hat. These moody guys with the guitars: do they just not bother listening to the weather forecast, or do they, like me, actually prefer Cairn Gorm when it's got the cloud down?

I thought I was all alone in the wind and mist, until there came a strange flash of light from behind the cairn. A Daddy, a Mummy, and an eleven year-old were taking a triumphant summit photo, the Daddy's camera not realising it was really daytime. Cairn Gorm in the mist is a slog, specially straight up alongside the funicular: well done, Eleven.

Seeking solitude on the summit of Cairn Gorm really is silly. Next came a long line emerging from the mist, more and more; no need to digitally multiply these, they'd do for the ghostly soldiers from *Lord of the Rings* just as they were. I stopped to chat with one at the back but immediately regretted it, as 'Oy! Hang On!' and the fifty in the mist had to stand in their boots while I made hill small talk about what they were up to. What they were up on was Cairn Gorm, and what they were up to was, being air cadets—and I guess Cairn Gorm is as high in the air as you can get without the expense of an aeroplane. Or perhaps it was a practical demonstration: pay attention lads, clouds can contain mountains.

A smaller party followed behind, a mere dozen or so, a fee-paying tour judging by the colour co-ordinated walking poles. 'Oh yes,' they said, irony dripping from their eyebrows like raindrops, 'we are enjoying it, we are enjoying it very much. The views are magnificent!'

Actually, the tops of Aladdin Buttress and Pygmy Ridge, cloud swirling between, these aren't bad at all, even if not the vista of Morlich, Nethy Forest, Moray Firth and the mountains of Caithness. I found the important little cairn sitting on its damp slab below Cairn Lochan, headed down over the edge, and tracked down the top of the Goat Track.

The Goat Track is good in the mist, with plenty of damp rocks and little gritty ledges, all this foreground interest brought out by a background of cloud. Below, the damp rocks levelled off to become Coire an t-Sneachda.

Those northern corries expose themselves recklessly to the travellers on the road alongside Loch Morlich. They show you everything they've got, and what they've got is a gentle hollow and a slim fringe of scrappy crag. Except that when you get in there, Sneachda has a splendidly unfriendly floor of bare boulders, and small pools of water, and a stretcher box to remind us of our mortality. Sunlit forests are a flat and far-below world glimpsed over the rim; on all other sides the boulders slope up to the feet of rocks that suddenly look serious. Remoter than it looks from Loch Morlich, it's still not quite a proper Scottish corrie, as it lacks a proper lochan. But the jaggedness of its granite reminds me more of the Tatras. It's one of the great places—and probably even more spectacular when you can actually see it.

Four more people came down the path behind me. Weaving among them were two smaller people. They were on their way back from Ben Macdui, by a route they hadn't quite intended. While Grandpa flagged a little, embarrassed by his bad compasswork, the two young people dashed ahead along the path, from time to time leaping into the air like over-excited gazelles. I couldn't catch the six year-old, so I tried my hill small talk on her slightly older sister. How had she found it up there?

'Was fun.'

'You didn't mind the mist?'

'Nope.'

'You didn't mind all those boulders?'

'Nope.'

Is it really correct to take an eight year-old and a six year-old up Britain's second highest mountain, in the mist, and subject them to an off-route boulderfield on the return? Evidently, it is.

Notes and references

(p38) 'Misty', originally recorded by the Erroll Garner trio and released on (appropriately) the 'Scenic Ridge' label, was remade by Johnny Mathis in 1959, when it reached No 12 in the UK charts. As the song belongs to five separate music companies, all now apparently defunct, I've not been able to clear the rights to quote the whole thing. This is a pity, as its insight on lost people following each other over the edge of Coire an t-Sneachda applies to the Macdui plateau just as much as to one's love life. 'Misty Lyrics' are easily findable on the Internet. Mark Knopfler ('the mist-covered mountains are home now to me') and Bob Dylan ('I've walked on the sides of twelve misty mountains') share this taste for tricky map-and-compass work.

(p38) The line from Verlaine resisted my attempts to track it down; in this it resembles that elusive cairn at the top of Fiacaill a' Choire Chais... But its spirit is found in *Torquato Tasso*: 'Le poète est un fou perdu dans l'aventure'. (The poet is a madman lost in some adventure.)

(p38) Clint Eastwood in the Oberland: the film was *The Eiger Sanction* (1975).

ROUTE 5 *Fiacaill Ridge*

Start: Coire Cas car-park
Distance to summit: 8km (5 miles)
Total ascent: 800m (2,700ft)

This is the Fiacaill Coire an t-Sneachda, a Grade 1 scramble, and not to be confused with the much easier Fiacaill a' Choire Chais to its east.

From the car-park corner, a wide, rebuilt path contours out right (west) signed for the Northern Corries. Take the second branch-path right, onto the foot of the Fiacaill Ridge. The ridge is stones, then easy level scrambling, to a rock tower. Take this direct, or more easily skirt to the right, up an enclosed corner, and then follow ledges to reach the crest above the steep tower. Follow the now-easier crest to the plateau.

Turn up right to the summit of Coire an Lochan. You could drop back east to the cairn of Route 2, or more wildly head south along the rounded, pathless crest directly to Lochan Buidhe to join the plateau path of Route 2 there.

How good? The scrambling is shorter than one would wish, but very enjoyable. In summer, and if you take the easier line, it's low in Grade 1 and only mildly exposed.

5 Snow Buntings

I strongly feel that our bird study is sublimated hunting, as is bird photography. All aspects of hunting: habitat selection, stalking our quarry, trying to outwit it, and finally experiencing intense satisfaction in getting what we want, are present in both bird watching and bird photography. I know through introspection that scientific bird study and bird photography give me exactly the kind of experiences and satisfactions as I once found in hunting seal on the arctic ice. It is subjectively the same to me whether I outwit the seal in order to shoot it or the bird in order to discover something about its behaviour. Even the trophy is an essential part of both. I am not in the least ashamed to confess that my photographs in this book are my trophies, and I am sure that my fellow bird watchers will agree with me.

Niko Tinbergen: *Herring Gull's World* (1953), quoted in *The Snow Bunting* by D Nethersole-Thompson (1966)

It's May of 1935. 'Fishface' and 'Annie' have been on the Macdui plateau for three days, and among the ten million boulders at the top of Garbh Uisge Mor have chosen the one that will shelter them through the summer. This is untypically far south for their species: they usually spend summer in Greenland.

They forage around the bases of old snowfields, where meltwater brightens the mosses and insects are out in the afternoon. They sit on the rocks in the evening sun, Annie admires Fishface in his handsome and appropriate outdoor clothing, and then they make love, for the first time, in their Cairngorms residency.

Four days later, 'Desmond' and 'Carrie' arrive on the plateau. They arrange their shelter in the open, half a mile away from Annie and Fishface, on a patch of gravelly grass. For their species this is an untypically high altitude, as they usually breed below the 300-metre contour. But for the next sixty-six days, they too will inhabit the plateau of Ben Macdui—this despite their greatly inferior shelter, which every storm threatens to destroy. Through long days of cloud, they lie in the centre of their covered area, shifting their bodies to avoid the drips, clinging to the supporting twigs to stop them snapping. It is not recorded that they mate, but presumably they do.

Carrie and her mate are less adapted to this world of grey stones and snow-patches than Fishface and Annie. Ill-equipped to exploit the insect eggs of the damp snowmelt patches, Desmond must descend to the valley for food. He lies up in the forest until dusk, and returns uphill unobserved by hostile gamekeepers. Some nights he doesn't get back at all, and Carrie must lie alone and hungry in her exposed shelter. By the end of the summer, Fishface and Annie have raised four young. Desmond, by contrast, has lost twenty percent of his body mass. But then, Desmond and Carrie are at a severe disadvantage up here. Desmond and Carrie are merely human. Fishface and Annie are snow buntings.

The snow bunting is a small bird shaped like a sparrow but more spherical, due to its greater depth of feather. The female is coloured in attractive pale browns, with a beige underside. In winter the male is more or less the same: the small, fluffed-out bird pecking for crumbs at the half-way station of the chairlift is a bunting, but could be of either sex. In the Cairngorms, though, the interesting buntings are the ones that spend the summer nesting season here; at this time the male is strikingly black-and-white.

Up as high as the 1,000-metre contour, the meadow pipit and wheatear do fly across the moorland. Above that level, the only small bird is the snow bunting. This makes it easy to identify even for the normally bird-blind. What's that small black-and-white bird perched on the summit cairn of Angel's Peak? You don't need your bird book: it's a bunting. On still days in May, the male's summer song twitters across the high corries.

The snow bunting's unique selling point is being the most hardy small bird in the world. In winter it joins the waders and others along the shorelines of northern Europe, or flocks in the old-fashioned sort of farmyards, but also finds food over moorlands, and around the middle station of the Cairn Gorm ski system. But during the summer nesting season it migrates, via Fair Isle, to northern Scandinavia and Southern Greenland. Buntings nest further north than any other land bird, even 200 miles from the North Pole. In the tundra, and on the Macdui plateau, they exploit the insect life of the damp snowfield margin, and the seeds of the newly uncovered grasses—away from the competition of other less insulated insect-eaters, and in territory where it's barely worthwhile for predators to come and hunt. Insects are carried up Macdui on warm breezes and get stuck in the melty bits at the edges of old snowfields. If the bunting does lose her eggs or chicks, she will usually try even further uphill, moving 100 metres higher up to reclutch.

The main predator is the weather. But eggs and chicks are also lost to stoats, voles and mice, and in the Arctic, to lemmings. Brown rats may follow humans' food scraps up the hill paths. All these are small enough to get to the nests inside the boulderfields. Out in the open, add the fox (in the Arctic, of course, this would be an arctic fox), the merlin and the peregrine. A snowy owl visited the Ben Macdui plateau in the 1950s, and must have found any buntings it managed to catch a nostalgic flavour of home.

In the Arctic, Eskimos in thick mist use the local accent of the bunting to work out where they are. With such a dense population, the main pressure on snow buntings is other snow buntings. Competition among males is formalised into the possession of territory, as it is with many birds. This means that as a cock bird you only need to fight at the edges, a great saving in energy, while prospective wives just have to eye up the real estate to assess your status.

In bunting terms Ben Macdui represents out-of-town rustic seclusion. There is far less pressure on territory, so a more free and easy pairing. 'Romeo' established two nest households and two wives, 'Mary' and 'Anna', 150 yards apart. After their first clutches he found a third, seducing the wife of a cock half a mile up the hill; the disconsolate cuckold being left with two fledglings to raise. (Marriage and seduction? These are the terms used by the two humans, crouched

48

in their home-made tent, watching through their binoculars the snow-bunting soap opera.)

The instincts and behaviour of the buntings are perfectly adapted to their lifestyle and environment. The same cannot be said for Desmond and Carrie Nethersole-Thompson, the observing humans. What are they up to?

Naturalist Nethersole-T started his career in boyhood, raiding a heronry in the treetops of Richmond Park. He describes the five centimetre-long dove-grey eggs as 'beautiful trophies of skill and daring'. In adolescence he graduated to the less accessible eggs of peregrines.

I do not regret that I first learnt to watch birds and to know birds as an egg collector. For some years I was a professional hunter. If I did not find, I did not eat; and neither did my family. We usually ate!

By the time he reached Ben Macdui he had abandoned nest-robbing, though the weekly Glenmore groceries were paid for out of the sale, for £100, of his existing egg collection. That must have come as a relief to the buntings of Scotland. Their first nest found, on Ben More Assynt in 1886, had its eggs stolen, blown, and presented to the Museum of Scotland. The first Cairngorm nest, in 1893, suffered a different fate; it had its eggs stolen, blown, and presented to the British Museum in London. But with the twentieth century comes the conservationist ethic. The naturalist Whitaker, in the Cairngorms in 1908, finds the eggs in his first bunting nest hardened and already dead. But luck is with him, and he comes across a second; he takes the five eggs to a little trickle of water to blow. But the third nest he leaves unattacked: 'One nest of a rare bird should suffice any naturalist. It certainly should a true lover of nature.'

N-T devotes several pages near the end of his book to explaining that the egg-collecting acts of himself and his wife did not endanger the buntings or reduce their overall breeding success. In fact it was commonplace for naturalists of the nineteenth and early twentieth centuries to combine a sincere and deep affection for the creatures they studied with at the same time shooting them to death. Naturalist Lionel Rothschild, of Tring in the Chilterns, sent collectors to Hawaii in the 1890s; there they extinguished about nine species including the greater koa-finch. In the southern USA, Bachman's warbler, thought extinct, was rediscovered by two separate naturalists in 1939: each of them repaired the error by shooting the bird.

We quite correctly mock such muddle-headedness—indeed, muddle-heartedness. Today we regard the natural world as pets rather than as prey. In our enlightened age, if a bird such as the ivory-billed woodpecker is rediscovered in the wild wood, we wouldn't ever shoot it. We would harass it to extinction with photographers, like Princess Diana.

It takes weeks of careful observation to hunt down a bunting; the Nethersole-Thompson family, over thirty years, two generations, and 263 tent nights, found just 38 nests. So while there are still egg-thieves, they aren't stealing the eggs of snow-buntings in Scotland. Instead, human beings are eliminating buntings in a more efficient and quicker manner altogether. Human-induced global warming means no more moist, insect-rich snow patches through the summer on the Macdui plateau. Often, all snow is gone by June. And next year, the year after, some year very soon, April will come and no snow buntings will sing above the granite boulders.

This year one of our liberal newspapers (*Independent on Sunday*, February 2007) devoted a global warming-themed travel supplement to the snowy places that are going to melt, the low atolls that are going to submerge, so as to suggest that before they disappear we should fly in large carbon-burning aircraft to visit them. We may be astonished and shocked by the bunting-loving egg-blowers. What future generations will mock us for will be our extraordinarily mild anxiety about global warming, nuclear proliferation, overpopulation and the extinction of tens of thousands of species.

That is, supposing there are future generations.

Notes and references

(p50) Desmond Nethersole-Thompson: *The Snow Bunting* (Oliver & Boyd 1966). He also wrote a book each about the dotterel and the Scottish crossbill.

(p51) The ivory-billed woodpecker, believed extinct since the 1940s, was rediscovered in Arkansas in 2004.

(p51) Snow bunting is *Plectrophenax nivalis*. The Royal Society for the Protection of Birds believes that 80–100 pairs currently nest in the Cairngorms area.

ROUTE 6 *From Aviemore by Lurcher's Crag*

Start:	Aviemore
Distance to summit:	20km (12½ miles)
Total ascent:	1,200m (4,000ft)

A bike path leads over the Spey on a former railway bridge. At Inverdruie turn south on paths (marked on Harvey's Cairn Gorm map) to Croft and Loch an Eilein. More forest paths lead by Achnagoichan, the Cairngorm Club footbridge, and Piccadilly (the path junction at NH938075) to Allt Druidh. In the jaws of the Lairig Ghru, double back left into Chalamain Gap, then head up the north ridge to Lurcher's Crag (Creag an Leth-choin). Continue south-east along the Lairig brink to Lochan Buidhe, to pick up the plateau path to the summit.

How good? The best routes start with some forest. This may be more forest than you want, unless you're really vigorous and fit.

6 Fairies

This hill, so regularly formed, so richly verdant, and garlanded with such a beautiful variety of ancient trees and thriving copsewood, was held by the neighbourhood to contain, within its unseen caverns, the palaces of the fairies: a race of airy beings, who formed an intermediate class between men and demons, and who, if not positively malignant to humanity, were yet to be avoided and feared, on account of their capricious, vindictive, and irritable disposition.

'They ca' them,' said Mr Jarvie, in a whisper, 'Daoine Schie, whilk signifies, as I understand, men of peace—meaning thereby to make their gude-will.'

Walter Scott: *Rob Roy* (1817).
The hill described is at Brig of Forth, Aberfoyle.

The fairies of the Gaelic lands—the Sith, pronounced 'Shee'—are not to be found dancing in the bowl of a primrose plant or flashing their legs below a sparkly see-through frock. Gaelic fairies are vicious, small-minded, and prone to take offence. Gaelic fairies are scary. And the Forest of Rothiemurchus is seriously infested.

For starters, fairies snatch away your lovely little newborn baby. This tendency was identified as far back as Persia in 3000 BC. Later, during a millennium of rapprochement between the two natures, the Indian Royal Family intermarried with fairies. Further west, however, the Ancient Greek 'Lamia' was the original sexy beast, part snake, part woman, her nipples dripping venom. You think it's colic or teething that makes your baby fractious? In fact she's become addicted to night feeds of this unwholesome stuff.

That is, if she's yours at all. The changeling is a wizened old immortal fairy pretending to be your baby. The sad fact is that, however ill-tempered and ugly the apparent infant, the fond parents still manage to get taken in. Folklore suggests: force the fairies to reconsider by exposing the nasty little creature in the forest for the time it takes a candle to burn down, or by holding its feet in the fire. This should oblige the fairies to reverse the swap.

Theologically, the fairies stand somewhere between the people and the angels. They are not fallen angels like Lucifer and Beelzebub who rebelled against the Godhead and are condemned to being the devils of Hell. It has however been suggested that, during that war in heaven, they were the ones that failed to sign up under Archangel Michael, instead standing prudently aside to see which side would win.

Fairies are vain, small-minded, capricious, cruel, deceitful and devoted to illusion. But they are not actually evil.

Richard Chaston (1620–1695) wrote that men and fairies both contain within them a faculty of reason and a faculty of magic. In men reason is strong and magic is weak. With fairies it is the other way round: magic comes very naturally to them, but by human standards they are barely sane.

(Chaston, who is not known to the British Library, appears in a footnote to page 299 of Susanna Clarke's *Jonathan Strange and Mr Norrell* 2004.)

And from the fairy point of view, human beings are insensitive, destructive and boringly incapable of any interesting magic. When they kidnap us away to their kingdom that lies on the other side of Hell—it looks like a flashy castle but it's actually just a hole in the hill—they are in fact doing us a big favour. Humans are just so damned serious about it all. Forget the boring day-job, the list of Munros that must be mounted. Loosen up, let out the magic, release the inner Faery. Dance all night to the thistle bagpipe, and all the day as well, and seven years until we dance our feet off onto our bloodstained bone-ends.

In Celtic tradition, fairies have been described as post-mortem existences of people who untimely died in battle or childbirth, or of unbaptised babies. But according to Susannna Clarke, who seems to know a lot about it, this is a misunderstanding. Those apparently deceased but actually taken away into Faery remain, to their discomfort and sorrow, human. An Orkadian witch had intercourse for three nights with her supposedly dead but actually fairified husband, and gained the unpopular power of identifying the paternity of unborn babies.

Pretty little fairies dancing about in bluebells were invented by Shakespeare—an Englishman who in his entire works only mentions mountains twice. In the early eighteenth century a Queen of the Fairies was put on display at Bartholomew Fair. She was a small black person who danced, perhaps a kidnapped African or Native American. Music hall fairies of the Victorian era, though necessarily human in size, wore costumes consisting of a couple of rose petals. You don't have to be a Victorian to understand that sex is dangerous—though being Victorian does help.

As for their houses, it is no use looking for them, because they are the exact opposite of our houses. You can see our houses by day but you can't see them by dark. Well, you can see their houses by

dark, but you can't see them by day, for they are
the colour of night, and I never heard of anyone
yet who could see night in the daytime. This does
not mean that they are black, for night has its
colours just as day has, but ever so much brighter.
Their blues and reds and greens are like ours with
a light behind them.

J M Barrie, author of *Peter Pan,* is very sound on
Fairies and their 'not actually nasty but certainly
not nice' natures. Consider his baby-snatched boys
in their underground home, their happy lives of
pointless frivolity, and the way that every Wendy
house is actually a tomb… However his fairylore may
not have been direct observation, but absorbed from
his Scottish nanny: a nanny whose duties included
guarding baby Barrie against being snatched into a
Fairyland of dead children who never grow up.

In February 2002 there passed me on a winter hilltop
something that sounded like a very small invisible
spaceship. It settled below the rim of the hill, the
noise now the flapping of a plastic sheet. I went to
peer over the edge, but there was a dodgy cornice.
A helicopter was searching the ridges at the time;
when I met the rescue men lower down, they told
me that someone had failed to turn up for work on

Monday, and an empty car had been found in the car-park. They sent their copter to search around my slope—for the sound could have been the lost man's bivvy bag, half-frozen in a drift. The evening was cloudless, the helicopter circled close: but of course found nothing.

While descending from Ben Macdui in October 1978, on a windy day with the cloud down, Ian Smith heard 'a loud whooshing noise ahead and to our left'. In a gap in the scudding cloud, he actually saw the cause: 'a projectile about the size and shape of a large tin of beans, hurtling at high speed vertically upwards'.

Such whooshing noises on hills were written about in *The Angry Corrie* in 2003; others besides myself have compared the sound with an invisible plastic bag. The explanations included meteorites, very tiny whirlwinds, and the sudden recrystallisation of snow. But the older inhabitants of Alvie (just south of Aviemore), in 1745, knew better. It was the *Sluagh*, the host of the air: the Faerie equivalent of EasyJet. And as for the car abandoned at the high car-park —anybody from Badenoch will have a fair idea what has become of the missing man.

For the Rothiemurchus Forest is a particularly bad place for Fairies. As you walk past the Toadstone that squats near Croft village to the north of Loch an Eilein, you may meet Bodach Lamh-dheirg, the red-handed spectre. He walks in a cloak with blood dripping from his fingers; if he meets you he will challenge you to fight and then kill you. There are the fairies who wash their green garments in Lochan Uaine; if they see you watching them as they do it, they will kill you. James Hogg has described their green hair, like seaweed, and their eyes small and black like the eyes of a codfish. It may be significant that Hogg survived the encounter to supply the only eyewitness description of the Ryvoan fairies: Hogg was already instructed in the safety procedures. His grandfather, the shepherd Will o' Phaup (William Laidlaw), was 'the last man of this wild region [that is, the Scottish Lowlands], who heard, saw, and conversed with the fairies'.

Hogg's is the only written description. But the 1928 SMC *Cairngorms* guide has a picture of a strangely-proportioned, cloaked figure stooping over Lochan Uaine. The caption and accompanying text don't mention the evident fairy captured by the camera. The writer, Sir Henry Alexander MA, LLD, presumably realised just how dangerous it would be to do so.

So what are the safety procedures James Hogg learnt from Grandpa Willy? Do not wear the fairies' colour green yourself, as this may offend them.

Carry small objects made of silver or of iron: old-fashioned rucksacks with their metal buckles may give some protection. And do not, when addressing your companions, speak their names aloud; this gives the fairies power. Really it's best to treat any green-haired stranger with respectful politeness, make one's excuses, in Gaelic of course, and leave.

Loch Avon is haunted by the Kelpie, or Water-horse. Climb on its back—and it's a tempting ride, the sports-car of horses—you can't climb off again, and it plunges deep into the loch and kills you. OK, a silver bridle could get you out of that one, but it's simpler just to leave the creature alone.

Lochan Uaine (SMC Cairngorms guide 1928)

But the main monster is Ferlas Mor, the Great Grey Man of Ben Macdui. In mist or moonlight, you hear his footsteps in the screes. For every three steps of your own, he takes just one, and a terror seizes you so that you run northwards over the stones until you reach Creag an Leth-choin, the Lurcher's Crag. And there you fling yourself over the edge to your death.

Enjoy your walk!

Notes and references

Historic faerielore from many sources, including *In Our Time*, Melvyn Bragg's programme on Radio 4, 11th May 2006.

(p57) The J M Barrie quote is from *Peter Pan in Kensington Gardens* (1906) available as ebook download from Project Gutenberg www.gutenberg.org

(p59) Ian Smith reported his experience with the *Sluagh* in *The Angry Corrie* January 2004. See also an article by Dougie Lockart in the issue for April 2003.

(p61) Lochan Uaine's fairy was snapped by J H Buchanan.

ROUTE 7 To Shelter Stone by The Saddle

Start:	Glenmore village
Distance & climb	15.5km (9½ miles)
(to Shelter Stone):	500m (1,700ft)

As on Route 1, take the track beyond Glenmore Lodge through the Pass of Ryvoan, forking right to the former site of Bynack Stable. After the footbridge over the River Nethy, a path, boggy at first, runs up the left (east) side of Strath Nethy and then to the left of the stream to The Saddle between Bynack More and Cairn Gorm. (From here you could head up carefully, as the slope has outcrops and, in winter, avalanches, onto Cairn Gorm to join Route 2.)

Descend a rough path to Loch Avon, and follow its west shore to its head. 400 metres up from the loch, Garbh Uisge is usually crossable at a small island, but not if it's in spate. The Shelter Stone is 200 metres due south, the largest of the boulders.

Routes 1, 8, 9 and 10 continue to Ben Macdui.

How good? This is shorter than Route 1 but the boggy bit in Strath Nethy is dispiriting. In reverse, it's the best bad-weather escape from Loch Avon.

7 The Wolfe Man

But still, these were the mountains of his fatherland that rose before his eye, and that name allied them to his heart by ties infinitely stronger than the tame surface of cultivation could have imposed. His soul soared aloft to the summits of the snow-topt Grampians, where the hardy and untameable spirit of Scotland seemed to sit enthroned among their mists, and to bid him welcome as a son.

Sir Thomas Dick Lauder: *The Wolfe of Badenoch,* Chapter XXIII. Sir Patrick Hepborne is heading north into the Cairngorms along with his faithful esquire Mortimer Sang and his mysterious, spunky, but at the same time somewhat soppy page Maurice de Grey. They will reach the Shelter Stone in Chapter XXVI.

In 1810 Revd Dr George Skene Keith made the first recorded walk up Ben Macdui. But within a very few years, or even a year or two before him, an ascent was made by one, not an earnest upper-middle-class divine but a light-hearted and charming minor aristocrat.

Tom Lauder in 1808 took up residence at Relugas, at the junction of the Findhorn and Divie rivers, thirteen miles north of Grantown: 'the prettiest place that ever was lived in', with tastefully laid paths and viewpoints.

In 1820 an uncle, Lord Fountainhall died, passing him a large inheritance and baronetcy; at which point he grew, as it were, his Dick. As well as landscaping his estate with its two pretty rivers and his 'small Scotch house' with its Italianate false front and tower, he spent daylight hours in rambles through Rothiemurchus, the Cairngorms and the wider countryside—in 1818 he discovered, and published the first account of, the parallel roads of Glen Roy. In the evenings, though, it was a life of music, silly games and amateur theatricals: 'a crowd of Popes, Cardinals, jugglers, gypsies, minstrels, flowergirls etc, the usual amusements of the family'—followed, once their ten children had gone to bed, by a few rubbers of whist. Both the Lauders were enthusiastic but bad singers. His wife, whose name was Charles Anne Cuming (presumably a Red Comyn of Badenoch) had 'the voice of a Clarion trumpet, much admired by some, though rather louder toned than pleased refined ears'.

We owe this description of them to their neighbour Elizabeth Grant, daughter of the Laird of Rothiemurchus, and author of *Memoirs of a Highland Lady*. She paints a delightful joint portrait of the Lauders. Since childhood the two had been intended for each other by their respective parents; as a natural result they grew up disliking one another intensely. Amid their constant quarrels, the one subject they could agree on was that they should never, never get married. 'How to avoid such a catastrophe was the single subject they discussed amicably. They grew confidential upon it quite, and it ended in their settlement at Relugas.' An Elizabeth-and-Darcy affair, indeed: and we recall that (as at Relugas) it is the tastefully laid-out paths and streams of Mr Darcy's Derbyshire estate that reveals him to the heroine and the readers of *Pride and Prejudice* as an OK chap. And maybe the new stagecoach service from Perth, thrice weekly from 1813, brought Jane Austen northwards over Drumochter to the Highland Lady who is her non-fiction equivalent.

If Elizabeth Grant wasn't quite the Jane Austen of Scotland, then her neighbour Tom Lauder wasn't quite Scotland's Walter Scott. And yes, that is unfair on Sir Walter, who could himself with some justice claim to be the Walter Scott of Scotland, being of the cattle-thieving Buccleuch tribe, deeply steeped in Scots history and language, and a collector of folklore in his native Selkirkshire. Even so, Walter Scott's habitat is Scotland interpreted for the English; Tom Lauder from Speyside comes across as more genuinely Scots than Scott. So while in *Rob Roy* Sir Wattie makes a tremendous fuss over some scenery alongside Loch Katrine, just outside Glasgow, Lauder takes us over Ben Macdui and into the heart of the Cairngorms. Undoubtedly he visited the Shelter Stone. We have his vivid description of a night underneath it in his *Wolfe of Badenoch*, with all the geography spot-on (apart from an intrusive glacier above Garbh Uisge). More: there is a drawing of it in his hand now in the Scottish National Gallery storerooms.

We have to mock him for describing the Macdui plateau as being obstructed by a glacier; but this detail in a perverse way adds to his plausibility. For he could scarcely have cribbed it from someone else, given that it's utterly untrue—but, on the other hand, a field of old hard snow, topped off with hoar frost, feels just like a glacier to a walker in a stiff breeze falling over on it.

The hero Sir Patrick Hepborne and his faithful but somewhat soppy page Maurice find an exciting path down to the Shelter Stone at considerably more than the Grade 2 scrambling of the Avon Slabs, so perhaps are misguidedly descending Afterthought Arête. Page Maurice makes heavy weather of it and gets carried down in his master's arms—which is bad practice even on simple scrambles, let alone Diff rock climbs like Afterthought Arête. Later, at the fireside,

Sir Pat gets treacherously attacked from behind with a big chunk of granite. Page Maurice revives in time to save him, then bursts into tears and retires to a dark corner. There's a further overnight knife-fight with a second invading Gael before everybody finally manages to get some sleep.

Here is the sensitive Maurice again, all eyes as he enjoys the Lairig Ghru by moonlight in Chapter LIV. Or rather she, Maurice being, as we suspected all along, a lassie in disguise. The Lady Beatrice, as he now is, camps at the northern entrance of the pass, with grumpy but faithful Rory Spears and harpist minstrel (or more accurately, doggerel-monger) Adam of Gordon.

'Tis a beautiful night, Adam,' said she; 'see how the moonbeam sleeps on the bosom of yonder little lake far up the pass. How dark do these masses of pine appear when contrasted with the silver light that doth play beyond them on those opposite steeps; how deep and impenetrable is the shadow that hangeth over the bottom far below us, where all is silent save the softened music of the stream murmuring among the rocks. But hark, what yelling sounds are these that come borne on the breeze as it sigheth up the pass?'

It is of course the sound of the wolves tearing to pieces a minor character for whom the author has no further use. And alas—how that doth the antique phrasing elongate without need the ardent and intermittently exciting tale! Were it not for the swounding and fainting, on each moment of wolfish howlings or valiant knightly setting to arms, of each and every feminine person within range of the author's pen, the long-drawn tale could lose some five score or more of its pages and be by that same extent the more readable…

The first fellwalkers of England were inspired by the romantic poets Coleridge and Wordsworth, and before them by landscape paintings of Italy brought back from the Grand Tour. Fellwalking in the south was a middle-class and poetic pursuit. In Scotland, however, Dick Lauder stands as the 'missing link' in the direct line between the cattle-thieves and marauding clansmen of the eighteenth century, and Queen Victoria on her pony.

If, as seems likely, he did overnight under the Shelter Stone, then he counts as its first respectable resident. But Dick Lauder, rambling in the forest of Rothiemurchus, is following the still-warm footprints of a recently-deceased marauder. His earlier novel *Lochandhu* (1825) is based on real-life Mackintosh of Borlum, as he knocks about in the woodlands of Rothiemurchus and Badenoch.

Brigadier Mackintosh of Borlum was the leader

who might have won the 1715 rebellion for the Old Pretender, if not for dithering and incompetent generals set over him. Obliged to surrender at Preston, he escaped from Newgate the night before his trial for high treason. He even gets a mention in Chapter 38 of *Rob Roy*: Di Vernon the (spunky, cross-dressing) heroine and her father served under him in this campaign.

Four years later, Borlum took part in the Battle of Glen Shiel, along with the real-life Rob Roy. After the war he became a dealer in black cattle, robber of travellers, smuggler of fine ruffled holland shirts, and presumably yet another resident beneath the Shelter Stone. He watched the cattle-thieves crossing the Tay: rifle in one hand held out of the water, the other hand grips the cow's tail, the pistol is between the teeth. And his aged widow, still living on Speyside, clearly knew where to lay her hands on the booty: according to Elizabeth Grant (1814), her 'handsome silks caused many a sly remark'.

'"Lochandhu" really was not bad,' wrote Elizabeth Grant; 'there were pretty bits of writing in it, but it was just an imitation of Walter Scott. I believe the book sold, and it certainly made the Author and his wife completely happy during its composition.'

The community that Lauder and Elizabeth Grant

lived in was still wrapped in the clan plaid; fifty years after Culloden, the gentry and the drovers danced reels together at the Pitmain Tryst near Kingussie, and Grant writes approvingly of 'feudalism'. But that plaid was already threadbare and unravelling; looking back from forty years later, her Journal observes sadly that theirs was the last generation of 'intercourse between the ranks, leading to a continuance of kind feelings', and adds sadly: 'the Highlands is not the Highlands now.'

They shared Rothiemurchus forest with the widow, at least, of the last authentic marauder. And they themselves, the first respectable hillwalkers, needed no instruction from the eighteenth-century landscape manuals or William Wordsworth. It was simply 'up late, a plentiful Scotch breakfast, [and] out all day'. For Eliza Grant, just like Dick Lauder, ran wild among the pine trees and islands of the Spey. Her mileages were shorter, as befitting her gender. Even so, her sister Mary almost managed to get drowned in the log flume set up by the timber men.

Later in life, Dick Lauder became Deputy-Lieutenant of Moray, Secretary to the Board of British White Herring Fishery and a Fellow of the Royal Society of Edinburgh. Liberal in his politics, he presided over what was then the largest ever outdoor rally, to promote the first Reform Bill of 1832 that started to widen the voting system. And five years before his death, when his own hill days must have passed, he was asked by Queen Victoria to write the official history of her first visit, the *Memorial of the Royal Progress in Scotland* (1843).

From her coach near Dunkeld the young queen had spotted the Grampians; Albert had admired them and said they looked a bit like Switzerland. And possibly her scribe Sir Thomas may have happened to mention, hidden beyond those slightly-Swiss foothills, the Shelter Stone, Loch Etchachan, and the granite crags of Ben Macdui. Sixteen years later, she would become the first reigning monarch to reach its summit.

Notes and references

(p65) Memoirs of a Highland Lady by Elizabeth Grant of Rothiemurchus (born 1795) covers the years 1797–1830, was written in Ireland 1845-54 and finally published in 1898. A one-volume paperback edition is published by Canongate Classics ISBN 978-0-86241-396-5.

(pp 64, 67-68) The Wolfe of Badenoch by Sir Thomas Dick Lauder (1827) is out of print but available secondhand. The Shelter Stone chapter is transcribed in SMCJ Vol XIV. I have not read *Lochandhu*; the 700 pages of *Wolfe* were reasonably enthralling but didn't leave me desperate for more Lauder.

ROUTE 8 *Coire Domhain*

Start:	The Shelter Stone
Distance to summit:	5km (3 miles)
Total ascent:	600m (2,000ft)

Use Route 1 or 7 to reach the Shelter Stone. Cross Feith Buidhe directly opposite the Shelter Stone and slant up left, on a faint path, to join the stream leading up into the shallow Coire Domhain. Head up left (west) to join the plateau path contouring south-west, to Lochan Buidhe and the summit.

How good? An easy way up Macdui, but less interesting than Loch Etchachan (Route 1). Also a way out from the Shelter Stone to Cairn Gorm or the high car-parks.

8 Keptie

*There is a fine line in climbing between the bold
and the self-destructive.*

David Roberts:
On the Ridge Between Life and Death (2005)

*The odds of being killed were about 1 in 10—a bit
daunting. But it mostly seemed to be happening to
Japanese climbers.*

Doug Scott (2006)
talking about the 1975 Everest South-West Face climb.

It's the Keptie Park in Arbroath, during one of those
proper winters we got in the 1960s, and two visiting
family members have taken the kiddies sledging.
Half the children of Arbroath are in the Keptie
Park, and the hill is well pisted, fast and firm, with a
comfortable run-out onto the level ground beside the
Keptie Pond.

The two responsible adults are called, for the
purposes of this chapter, Cousin Andrew and Cousin
James. They find it frustrating to stand and watch the
downhill action. Once we the wee ones start to flag,
they decide it's their turn. They climb on, their feet
on the metal runners, their big adult knees sticking

out sideways. We give them a hearty push. With skilful balance—both of them are competent rock climbers—they manage to stay upright on the high and narrow sledge.

Larger bodies are less affected by air resistance. At impressive speed, they shoot across the level ground at the bottom and out onto the Keptie Pond. The pond, as they career across it, makes cracking noises and groans; it also appears, mysteriously, to be gradually rising alongside the sledge. At the exact centre of the pond the sledge slows—comes to a stop—and sinks into the chilly water.

The two cousins sit waist-deep in the Keptie Pond, while the children of Arbroath stand alongside and marvel: 'Ye've fa'en in!' The cousins try by gestures to persuade the children to stand and laugh at them from a slightly safer distance. And they remember, perhaps, a similar incident in the Cairngorms from several years before.

None of this 'long walk in' nonsense in those days, and no mountain bikes either: they drove up the track from Linn of Dee and parked at Derry Lodge. Cloud was above the tops, snow was on the slopes. Unfortunately, out of the former and into the latter was falling a fair amount of rain; it was no day for a climb. They settled on a simple walk to Ben Macdui. Having got there, invigorated by the chilly wind, they decided to continue across the plateau to Cairn Gorm.

Now from Cairn Gorm, the journey back across the plateau would be head-to-wind, with sleet soaking into the woolly mittens and slipping between the woolly jumper and the cotton anorak. This would not be altogether enjoyable. Loch Avon, on the other hand, in its deep hollow between the hills—Loch Avon with the square-topped Shelter Stone Crag dropping splots of wet snow 200 metres into the boulderfield, and the spate streams dancing among the boulders, and grey snowclouds dashing from the Stag Rocks to the Black Stacks in thirty seconds or less—that certainly is enjoyable. It was 3.00pm, and the heavy cloud-cover meant that the light was already starting to go. The direct, and what's more the sheltered, way back to the Derry is by Loch Avon and Loch Etchachan.

So from Cairn Gorm they descended into the shallow bowl of Coire Raibert, and followed its busy stream over the rim and down towards Loch Avon. On the way down the small, stony path, Cousin Andrew (the elder of the two) may have been considering the best way around Loch Avon. With rain falling into thawing snow, the River Avon at the foot of the loch would be in yellow spate with the boulders rumbling underneath. At the loch's head, the combined stream of Garbh Uisge and Feith Buidhe would also be high: on a bad day walkers here have been forced half-way back up Ben Macdui before getting across it.

They arrived at the loch shore and looked across to where the steep path zigzags up to Loch Etchachan. And maybe the spate streams and the humiliating re-ascent were in his mind, but it was in a cheerful voice that Cousin Andrew made his suggestion: 'the easy way here; simply straight on across the loch'.

Loch Avon

Loch Avon is half a mile across: a fifteen-minute walk at most. If there were any mishap, the closest telephone would be at Glenmore, eight miles away on the opposite side of Cairn Gorm. But who thinks mishap? They set out across ice turned slushy-grey by the rain.

Later I asked the younger of them about this. 'Well,' he said, 'Cousin Andrew is a member of the Scottish Mountaineering Club. So, of course, I assumed he knew what we were doing.'

Loch Avon in the middle is 20 metres deep. As they passed over this point they were wading in warm water up to their ankles on top of the ice. By then there was no point at all in turning back (and anyway, Cousin Andrew is a member of the Scottish Mountaineering Club…) A human being in ice-cold water survives about a quarter of an hour. Did they sensibly separate—or did they walk together, both across or else both in at once, and nobody ending up as a sole survivor with the awkwardness of having to tell the other one's wife?

Not at all, says Cousin Andrew. 'It never entered our heads that what we were doing could be considered at all risky, or at least no more risky than rock climbing normally is. The point is that we had walked up Cairn Toul and Braeriach the previous day and were a bit weary and wanting to get back and our boots off and dinner. And may I point out that Cousin James, as you call him, was actually a member of the Alpine Club.'

The ice held. And really it would have been a nuisance, diverting all the way back up the Feith Buidhe.

ROUTE 9 Avon Slabs

Start:	The Shelter Stone
Distance to summit:	3.5km (2 miles)
Total ascent:	600m (1,900ft)

Two streams, Feith Buidhe and Garbh Uisge Beag, join just above the head of Loch Avon. Between them there sweeps down a spread of glacier-smoothed slabs, becoming steep at the foot. The scramble avoids these lower, steeper slabs by way of the bed of Garbh Uisge Beag, the stream on the left. Follow the stream bed to the base of a waterfall. Take the clean rocks immediately to the stream's left (Grade 2), or broken ground further left (Grade 1), until level with the top of the steeper slabs. Now broad footholds lead through the stream just above a pair of waterfalls—avoid this, obviously, if the stream is in spate.

Walk out right, to the centre of the slabs. Above, a band of steeper rock comes in from the right and dwindles to nothing in the centre. Take this near its left end (Grade 1) or further right where it's higher (Grade 2). Walk right, half-way to the bounding Feith Buidhe stream, then head up to the left of a trickly stream (Grade 1)—or assault the steeper rocks further left (Grade 2). Walk on up gentler

On the Avon Slabs

slabs to find a break in the short final steepening.

Head south across the shallow upper corrie of the Garbh Uisge Beag, and over North Top to the summit.

How good? A first-rate mountaineering scramble, Grade 1 or 2 depending on route chosen.

9 Hobnailed Notions

Cragging and bagging around the five fourthousands

> *It is now possible to become a 'good climber'*
> *without ever going to the mountains, or even to*
> *the gritstone edges of Derbyshire. Climbing walls*
> *can be fun, yet the times I still enjoy most revolve*
> *around climbing in beautiful or unusual places,*
> *climbing with good friends—perhaps when things*
> *don't go exactly to plan.*
>
> Paul Dearden: *Classic Rock Climbs (1994)*

'Where do true ideas come from?' Chairman Mao asks us in his Little Red Book. 'Do they fall from the sky? No. True ideas come from three things.' It's not one of Mao's most inspiring passages, and while the first two sources of truth were the struggle of the Proletariat and scientific research, I can't remember the third one at all. However, it almost certainly wasn't 'grow a beard and read old guidebooks of the Scottish Mountaineering Club'.

The old and bearded idea of hillwalking was that it should include a little bit of rock wherever rock is offered. The old and bearded idea of rock climbing was that it should include a walk over the summits. Mao's words floated through my mind on meeting up with my half-sister and her boyfriend in the Cairngorms. These young people, who only took to the rocks two years ago, seem to have absorbed the antique attitude that climbing takes place on or near mountaintops, up pathetically easy places (they've invented seven new grades of difficulty since I used to do it), and is followed by some high-level hillwalking. This is the early twentieth-century game, but they can't have it from our Dad, who stopped climbing before Barbara was born.

Climbing Alpine-style in the Himalaya means no fixed ropes, no big rucksacks, quick and risky. Climbing antique-style in the Cairngorms requires the same jump of the imagination and the same lightweight overnights: in this case, the Shelter Stone and the Garbh Choire refuge. It means going up all five of the fourthousanders, on absurdly easy rock, with rucksacks, over a long weekend.

So it was that I found myself climbing big Cairn Gorm by a small and surprising route called Pygmy Ridge, created by Harold Raeburn in an uncharacteristic moment of levity (for Raeburn's more typical grimness see Chapter 10). The first shock was Coire an t-Sneachda. Rock walls rose on either side, and the bottom was rocks tumbled in piles, and like most Sneachda visitors we were suspecting that the place must be even better if you could see it. We boulderhopped between two of the misty lochans, carefully didn't comment on the sinister stretcher box, and then scrambled by gully and grass and gentle spurs up the complicated headwall, looking for our ridge.

Sneachda headwall, in cloud, is a journey that swaps around the real world and the virtual. We fumbled around trying to read half-seen patches of gully, grass and gentle rocks, while the true travel took us up the paper diagram in our Dad's old guidebook. Soon we reached the point on the page where the dotted route-line began; marked in the real world by a trampled place and a rising rock.

Pygmy Ridge starts off steep: could this mist-swathed precipice really be seven grades easier than Ride the Wild Surf? It could. It began on very big holds, easier than it looked, and then just got even less difficult as it went up.

Paul Dearden's book, quoted at the top of the chapter, is promoting just such gentle old-fashioned mountain explorations. Except that it actually contains nothing easier than E3 (eight grades harder than Pygmy Ridge), nothing less recent than 1980 (Pygmy Ridge is from 1905), and nothing at all in Scotland. Even England's Lakeland is represented by Hodge Close Quarry, which, so far from being a mountain crag, is actually underground. And when you've looked at his pictures of Ride the Wild Surf (one pitch, 150 feet, E4 6a in Dinorwig slate quarries, bolted and with some artificial holds) you realise why many climbers can't be bothered with the two-hour walk, uphill all the way, for the absurdly easy Pygmy Ridge of Cairn Gorm.

Soon Pygmy stopped even pretending to be serious, and relented into a picturesque arête. This got even prettier as we emerged above the cloud into bursts of sunshine. Finally, like the spirits of sweet little dead babies arriving in Heaven, we stepped gently along the last cloud-hung boulders and down onto the Cairngorm plateau.

The next climb-time, an evening excursion from Loch Avon, promised to be slightly less titchy than the Pygmy. The approach, a pleasant ramble across The Terrace, would place us above some sort of a drop for the climbing of an open corner on large holds at the same grade of Moderate. The Battlements is a creation of the famous Dr Tom Patey, a useful descent route from his more demanding climbs alongside.

The inappropriately named Terrace turned out to be steep moss dropping softly over the top edge of the bottom two-thirds of Carn Etchachan Buttress. And the thing about the climb itself is this: Patey was the GP in Ullapool, but that was a bit of a deception, as he was actually a dour Aberdonian. Accordingly, the climb was described with Aberdonian nonchalance so as not to spoil our exploratory pleasure. I followed my two leaders by their footprints on the deep mossy holds, up into a greasy corner below a short but slightly over-hanging wall. The handholds here were not quite right. Fortunately there was protection from a slightly rusted nut. The nut was good, fallen-off-on and jammed in by previous adventurers. And Matt coped, Barbara coped on a tight rope, I coped on a tight rope too.

When an Aberdonian called a route Mod, didn't I hear that he actually meant Diff or V Diff? And do I further remember, as a young and press-ganged guidebook writer, re-grading T Patey and C Bonington on Cioch Nose Direct, of Applecross? I've looked it up, and indeed 'the Diff to end all Diffs' (Bonington and Patey 1960) became Hard V Diff (youthful guidebook co-author 1973) and finally Severe (SMC *North-West Highlands* guide 2004).

On the way down the young folk climbed the Forefinger Pinnacle. I could have climbed it too, or taken photos of it; but not both, as evening had arrived and the light was going. I chose to take the photos, and Matt obligingly posed on the very tip

Forefinger Pinnacle

top rock. 'Very nice son,' says his mother on receiving my picture, 'and whatever happened to your helmet?' Meanwhile his friends see the same picture in *Trail* magazine, and send mocking emails because of his knees being very slightly bent.

Even in Scotland, in August, if you keep climbing long enough the day does eventually end. We scrambled down Pinnacle Gully, stones and wildflowers and a little bit of bare rock, as it gradually filled up with darkness and the loch below us went silvery-grey.

The Shelter Stone is half-full of ancient tea bags and orange plastic, and stuffed to the doorway with history—its first reputed sleepover was in the late fourteenth century by Alexander Stewart, Alisdair Mor mac an Righ (Big Alex the king's son), called the Wolf of Badenoch. Provided you don't live in the late fourteenth century yourself, the Wolf is a splendid fellow, reinforcing Loch an Eilein castle, playing chess with the Devil, and burning down Elgin cathedral in reprisal for an annoying excommunication by the Bishop. Midges lurk in great numbers in the Shelter Stone's low doorway but for some reason don't come inside: perhaps it's the orange plastic that puts them off, or maybe they're afraid of biting us in case we might be Big Alex of Badenoch and bite back.

In terms of routes up Ben Macdui, the Avon Slabs are the one with the hobnails and the big beard. Some might consider the start-point, at the head of Loch Avon, inconvenient. But this is nonsense, as it's just ten minutes away from the Shelter Stone. Nice clean granite is underfoot, all graded between not-very-difficult and a-lot-easier-than-that, and views are all the way along Loch Avon. The Garbh Uisge has to be crossed at a point above its first waterfall—well it doesn't have to be, technically speaking, but some lines have that ineluctable imperative, as large flat footholds lead through a slightly splashy cataract with plenty to hold on to but a couple of waterfalls below to get swept away down. The camera stayed dry—it'd have been a shame to have lost the Forefinger Pinnacle photos.

The rock slabs and scrambling account for a height gain of fully 300 metres. The rest of the way is along one of those grassy valleys with a small stream that rather resemble Yorkshire except for being at 1,200 metres. And all the people around the big cairn on Ben Macdui, relaxing limply under blue skies and a torrid sun, are wondering how we've managed to reach that point soaked to the skin.

Cairn Toul is not a climbers' mountain. However, its outlier the Angel's Peak has a ridge that's Alpine in atmosphere even if only Munro-bagger in difficulty. From the Garbh Choire shelter, a path leads up steeply between a slabby, splashy stream and a bit of broken rock. At the top, suddenly, is the Lochan Uaine, the green lochan; one of four so named in the Cairngorms. From there it's clambering over boulders, and a gently-angled slab with big holds and the merest whiff of exposure, and little ledges with grass, and great views right across the Lairig Ghru to Ben Macdui, and right across the Garbh Choire to the rocks of Braeriach.

At the top, the sun had collapsed tiredly into a cloudbank away over the Great Moss, and the midges had come out to dance in the dusk. Given that the summit of Angel's Peak is above 1,200m, presumably the little grey midge-wings were at that moment beating over every square metre of Scotland. Fortunately, some lover of humanity had left midge-coils at the Garbh Choire refuge.

A walkers' guidebook, which is what I was writing that summer, doesn't really need Moderate rock climbs that are actually V Diffs; so I retired from the rockface and took long-focus photos of the young people from various directions. The actual reason for me not being on Domed Ridge and taking photos from close up, was the previous climb on Carn Etchachan. But it was all very thrilling anyway. '600ft, Moderate', it said in the old book. From the summit of Braeriach I watched with mixed emotions as Matt led what was certainly a V Diff move, superbly exposed, a long way above his runner. The hand that goes pat pat pat seeking the essential handhold that isn't actually there—this is usually a private moment, but not on the final pitch of Domed Ridge, in full view from Braeriach's cairn across 40 metres of empty air. The move up the final slab, he told me later, had started easily enough…

We took a long time to emerge from Coire Bhrochain, enjoyed the fading of the day from the ridge of Braeriach, and arrived in Aviemore early enough to find a bunk in the youth hostel, or a meal at the Indian restaurant—but not early enough to do both these things. It was the meal that mattered. And so I ended in my bivvy bag in Rothiemurchus forest, where I could only sleep facing in-the-way, towards the dark trees. For looking outwards at the starlit sky gave the unsleepable sight of several thousand midges, an inch away outside the midge net. For the first (and I passionately hope, the last) time ever I could actually hear midges: a gentle hum of 10,000 wings, somewhere near Middle C. They stay around for the Braemar Games, first Saturday in September, in the hope of biting Her Majesty.

History tends to cycles—Chairman Mao as a sound Marxist-Leninist would have to agree. The first time it comes as climbing, the second as something else. As rock climbers move ever upwards in a puff of white chalk in the direction of Ride the White Surf, there's invented a new sport for walkers called 'Scrambling'. Scrambling is walking with the use of the hands but without a climbing rope, given that a climbing rope makes it climbing. And so grade Moderate is renamed as 3(S); and Pygmy Ridge gets into my walking book after all.

Then, in a further twist of the dictionary, our safety-conscious age commends, for scrambles of Grade 2 and 3, not to mention 3(S), a rope.

Just change the name, and let's get on with the game.

Notes

The routes were: Pygmy Ridge (Moderate) to Cairn Gorm; The Battlements (undergraded Moderate); Forefinger Pinnacle (Moderate); Avon Slabs (scramble Grade 2) to Macdui; NE Ridge Angel's Peak (scramble Grade 1) to Cairn Toul; Domed Ridge (Diff) to Braeriach. Another time I'd omit The Battlements, scramble Cairn Toul's east ridge (Grade 1), then descend the ridge of Angel's Peak.

In the 1960s, Malcolm McArthur and Sandy Paine combined five classic Severe ridges with their five summits in a two-day trip: Eagle Ridge to Lochnagar, Mitre Ridge to Beinn a' Bhuird, Snake Ridge to Beinn Macdui, Sphinx Ridge to Braeriach and Roberts Ridge to Sgoran Dubh Mor. Savage Slit would be the way up Cairn Gorm, but Cairn Toul doesn't have great climbs at this standard (or, indeed, any other above scrambling Grade 1). (Scottish Hill Runners' website).

ROUTE 10 *Forefinger Pinnacle and Gully*

Start: The Shelter Stone
Distance to summit: 4km (2½ miles)
Total ascent: 600m (2,000ft)

Contour west for 50 metres, then go up grassier ground among the stones to the base of the tremendous Shelter Stone Crag. Head right, into Pinnacle Gully. Go up this, choosing bare rock rather than scree, passing to the right of the Forefinger Pinnacle. This can be climbed by the arête of its lower, uphill, side (Moderate, or Grade 3 scramble, ferociously exposed).

A final wet wall behind the pinnacle is climbed on the right. The slope above is scree on rock; use the stream-washed bare rock, or else handholds in the right-hand wall, to emerge onto the plateau.

Head left along the crag tops to Carn Etchachan, then south-west over little-trodden plateau to North Top and the summit.

How good? A rather scrappy Grade 1 scramble, with the embellishment of a short but fearsome Moderate climb. The gully route is done for its atmosphere and situations rather than its technical interest.

10 Dour Aberdonians
and the badness of granite

The theme of our conversation was the irrational preference that most men betray for clean, sound rock. 'Any fool can climb good rock,' said Dr J H B Bell, as our car topped the Devil's Elbow and nosed down towards Braemar, 'but it takes craft and cunning to get up vegetatious schist and granite.'... We were bound for Lochnagar—the greatest citadel of vegetatious granite.

W H Murray: *Mountaineering in Scotland* (1947)
The climb described was in May 1939.

Joe Brown
Look down
From your pillar of fame
Cairngorm Tiger is my name

Tom Patey: *One Man's Mountains* (1971)

Some ways of going up hills are more fun than others. We came from under the Shelter Stone to find two inches of wet snow. We were cold already—a night in wet sleeping bags had seen to that—but soon we were going to be colder. We had not brought spare jerseys, it being the month of June (ah, but June on Ben Macdui). Our packs had been filled with food

94

at Ballater for the long crossing to Kingussie, and were heavy; the sleet falling onto them was soaking in nicely to make them heavier still. After five days afoot our feet were sore, but Ben Macdui's boulders were soon to make them sorer.

A lapping sound in the mist was Loch Etchachan, and then we saw it: grey water, rippling under the wind, each white blot of sleet abruptly extinguished as it silently hit the surface. As we moved out of the loch's hollow, the wind strengthened. Uphill, our exertions kept us warm. On the plateau, nine inches of new snow lay over the stones. The Sappers' Hut appeared, its upwind side splatted white. We crouched behind the cairn and took the bearings for the top of the Tailors' Burn.

Level ground brings less self-generated heat; level ground upwind brings sleet into the hood of the anorak and down the front of the neck. We found the Tailors' Burn, by stepping into it through the snow. Downhill now, on still steeper boulders, I realised that any more map reading was going to stiffen my fingers and stop them holding the compass. But downhill was the Lairig Ghru; it would not still be snowing down in the Lairig Ghru. And once down, we could abandon our plans for the eventual west coast and Isle of Skye, simply turn right and head out to Aviemore and the railway station. (Although, it being the month of June, the train would probably be unheated.)

Some ways of going up hill are more fun. Others are fun so subtle that it could almost be mistaken for suffering. But we've a grand talent for forgetting; as when, half way down to the Lairig Ghru, the clouds open to a blue sky, the sun appears, and we eventually reach Kingussie at 9.00pm, still damp but at the same time sunburnt.

When it comes to fun, Scottish Winter Climbing is one of the most subtle forms of fun available anywhere. It is also, in these days of sport climbing and indoor climbing and modern protection methods, refreshingly dangerous.

Mountaineering came late to the Cairngorms. The first climbs in Scotland were on Skye, at that time conveniently accessible by steamer from Glasgow. By the turn of the twentieth century, the main Nevis ridges had been climbed by Norman Collie and Harold Raeburn; but apart from a couple of lines on Lochnagar nobody had climbed the granite and ice of the east. The Cairngorm Club, founded in 1887 under the Shelter Stone, was initially for walkers and naturalists.

Even with the coming of the motor car to the mountains, Cairngorm climbing was notable only for the fact that there wasn't any. The granite was simply the wrong sort of stuff. As the first SMC guide *The Cairngorms* (1928) pointed out:

> *The granite weathers along horizontal and vertical lines of weakness, giving the cliffs the appearance, in places, of gigantic masonry, the upper blocks of which become in time more and more undercut until they finally collapse. The rounded edges and absence of clean-cut fissures render the Lochnagar rock unfavourable to climbing.*

Ben Macdui was just as bad:

> *The cliffs of the Coire Sputan Dearg at the head of the Luibeg form the largest rock face on Ben Macdhui, but, like most of the granite in the Cairngorms, the rock is not suited for climbing, being rounded and devoid of holds.*

So that guidebook mentioned no climbs in Coire Sputan Dearg, and only three in the whole Greater Macdui area between the Lairig an Lui and the Lairig Ghru. We know, because he was chased off it by the Great Grey Man, that Collie was on the mountain. Maybe he kept his resolve never to revisit Ben Macdui: at any rate, he did no noteworthy climb on either rock or snow. That there are any climbs at all is down to one man.

Harold Raeburn

Even if he has rather fewer hill features named after him than Norman Collie, Harold Raeburn still has plenty, including one important buttress on Ben Nevis and another on Lochnagar. He was the outstanding Scottish climber of the years before the First World War, when technical clothing meant stout Harris tweed with shirt and tie, and boots were soled with farm-labourer type hobnails and soft iron clinkers. He made the first ascents of Observatory Ridge and Buttress on Ben Nevis (1900-01)—climbing solo. This may have been out of altruism: the technique of the time, using rope lengths of 30 feet and direct belays over spikes of rock, meant that if the leader fell, so did anybody tied to him.

Raeburn's winter ascents of Crowberry Gully on the Buachaille and Green Gully on Nevis were conveniently forgotten by the following generation, who would not have been capable of them; they were omitted from guidebooks and waited thirty years for second ascents. Living in Edinburgh, Raeburn made illegal ascents on Salisbury Crags, but he was also one of the first to climb without a guide in the Alps. He achieved nine first ascents of mountains in the Caucasus, before an adventurous journey back across Europe in the opening days of the Great War.

He was chosen as the mountaineering leader of the Everest expedition of 1921. But although supremely talented and fit, at fifty-six he was just too old, and dropped out with dysentery before reaching the mountain. This was just as well, as he was arguing all the time with the overall leader (Lt-Col Howard Bury) and getting on George Mallory's nerves as well. Fifty-three-year-old Alexander Kellas had survived his encounter with the Grey Man of Macdui (see Chapter 16) only to die on the same expedition. Raeburn recovered, rejoined the expedition, and reached 6,700 metres below the North Col; but the effort finished him as a mountaineer. Before dying

On Pygymy Ridge

four years later he may have lost his wits along with his fitness, as he came to believe that he'd murdered Alexander Kellas.

Strangely, that 1928 *Cairngorms* guide fails to mention the very first route in the area, Raeburn's charming Pygmy Ridge in the northern corries of Cairn Gorm. He climbed it in 1904; I repeated it a century later (see Chapter 9).

Apart from the scrambles on Forefinger Pinnacle and the Fiacaill Ridge, the only other routes known in 1928 are on the formidable Shelter Stone Crag. On June 16th 1907, with F S Goggs as his intrepid second, Raeburn climbed down this face immediately to the west of Castlegates Gully by the 200-metre Castle Wall route, taking fifty-five minutes over it. It's graded Diff (in ascent), with much scrambling in the upper part but 'mildly difficult' lower down. (A half-century later the 1961 *Climbers' Guide* was to say: 'more than one awkward pitch, and the rock should be handled carefully'.)

This was just the warm-up, a way to reach the foot of the crag. They then re-ascended the crag further to the right, by a 200-metre route now called Raeburn's Buttress and graded Severe. 'The rock is good, but the holds apt to be obscured by moss and earth,' wrote Raeburn. The 1961 Guide is more respectful:

'All the 500 feet up to the square-cut shoulder is on extremely steep rock veiled with vegetation... The crux is especially dangerous.'

The area guidebook's second edition of 1938 repeats the dismissive remarks about the rounded holdless unclimbability of the Cairngorms, but now with an appendix listing six climbs on Lochnagar's unfavourable rock, together with one on Creag an Dubh-Loch. As for the Macdui plateau, Coire an Lochan now has several climbs. Plus, on the north side of Beinn a' Bhuird, a climb called Mitre Ridge.

Fun in gullies

Erase Harold Raeburn, and the early routes in Scotland are almost all in gullies. In gullies one might find good snow, of the sort they get in Switzerland. Gullies are comforting to be in: 'If we all slipped, there was a satisfaction in knowing where we should roll to, and the chances were greatly in our favour of stopping somewhere before we reached the bottom.' (F S Goggs, presenting himself as a somewhat reluctant third-on-the-rope behind Raeburn in 1902.)

Tom Patey summarises the pleasures of such places in winter conditions: 'The highlight of the gully climb was the Ice Pitch, followed by some good old-fashioned fun at the cornice. Such a climb was remarkably lacking in variety.' But the Cairngorm gully in summer was even more distinctive:

Most gullies are unpleasant. A Cairngorm gully is doubly so. It is the sort of place you would incarcerate your worst enemy; a dank gloomy prison where moisture seeps from every fissure and 'all the air a solemn stillness holds'—save for the constant drip, drop from many a greasy moss-enshrouded chockstone and the occasional dull thud as another ledge sloughs away in a welter of slime and rubble.

But all that was about to change. The 1928 guidebook carried two pictures of 'a great ridge of sheer rock, 600 feet high' in the Garbh Choire of Beinn a' Bhuird. One sunny day in 1933 two parties arose from their bivouacs in the corrie, took a quick dip in the stream, and climbed the Mitre Ridge by two separate routes: Direct Route (Hard Severe in nails) and the Cumming-Crofton Route (Severe). Two months later, an ill-informed Mr Charles Ludwig arrived to make what he believed was a first ascent (climbing in socks). Suddenly, the unfavourable granite had come good.

Some of what had happened was better roads, cheap second-hand motor cars—the one that drove to Tomintoul in 1933 had 'string and wire strengthening'. Climbing boots had lost their welts, and carried serrated hard nails called Tricounis that allowed the sole-edge to be placed on small holds. Windproof anoraks and lightweight tents had been developed on the Everest expeditions of the 1920s. Rope-lengths had extended to 60 feet and more. Shoulder belays and anchors had replaced the inadequate direct belay.

But the main novelty was a generation of young climbers out of Glasgow: the most notable, because of his inspiring book about it all, being W H Murray. *Mountaineering in Scotland* (1947) describes the use of the head torch for finishing off an all-day ice-climb, the slaters' pick, the noble art of step-cutting up steep ice where the absence of a satisfactory belaying technique meant 150-foot unprotected run-outs: 'Many a new ice climb was made because the leader *had* to go on,' wrote Jimmy Marshall (SMCJ 1961).

The campaign opened in Glen Coe, with its new road (built 1922), and on Ben Nevis with its convenient CIC Hut. It took the Aberdonians, with their temperamental affinity with the gritty grey stuff, to open up Britain's most uncompromising rock routes, and to discover that appreciable amounts of ice could indeed be found on Lochnagar.

The arrival of the Aberdonians
The Scots word 'dour' (from the French *dûr*, hard)

103

means uncommunicative, grim, stern. It describes equally the inhabitants of Aberdeen, their cold granite city, and the cold granite rocks they climbed. As they occupied the choice fireside chairs in Bob Scott's barn bothy at Luibeg, 'these men spoke of icy vigils and gigantic ice falls; routes that finished long after dark; remote bivouacs in far-away corries'.

In 1941 the editorship of the SMC Journal passed to an Aberdonian, J H B Bell. He used its pages to praise, in an oblique Aberdonian way, the Cairngorm granite.

> *Granite climbing is by no means easy, for the crags, at first attempt, may appear to offer very little between easy scrambling and vertical walls of imitation masonry. There is much loose rock in many places, and the rounded edges offer few belays... Vegetation is often found on ledges and in chimneys and cracks, but this is avoidable and not at all troublesome... The granite is often coated with a thin green or greenish-black patina of lichen which becomes very slippery when wet.*

As a direct result of such praise disguised as faint damnation, it was discovered that the rocks of Coire Sputan Dearg are not after all unsuitable for climbing. By 1948 it was the most popular corrie in the Cairngorms (outside of Lochnagar) due to its sunny aspect and its walk-in of a mere two hours from Derry Lodge. It was the classic Snake Ridge (450 feet, Hard Severe by Bill Brooker, 1949) that my father was aiming for in this book's Chapter 13 when he lost one of his watches. Then, in 1949, the huge crag of Coire Etchachan, the one Queen Victoria passed under in 1859, was abruptly discovered.

It suited the Aberdonians just fine to talk down what they themselves wanted to climb up. Next door to the Shelter Stone Crag is another, slightly less intimidatingly steep, but even larger. Mac Smith told Tom Patey that Carn Etchachan 'was all rotten and loose and were it otherwise it would have been climbed long ago'. The ploy was counter-productive; Patey was, after all, another Aberdonian. He immediately suspected a fine unclimbed crag and set off at the first snowfall to find it.

The resulting route, Scorpion (1952), actually received its first summer ascent retrospectively, seven months after Patey's winter ascent. Within the next few years this virgin crag would be networked with routes for both winter and summer conditions, climbed mainly by Patey—with The Battlements (Chapter 9) as a handy way off. Meanwhile on the other side of the Pinnacle Gully, and forty years after Raeburn, the Shelter Stone Crag had received its

third route (Clach Dhian Chimney, V Diff, 1947).
By 1958 Patey and friends were to add three more.

Tom Patey
Because he lived and climbed on the 'wrong' side of
the Devil's Elbow, the phenomenal Tom Patey has
been underestimated. At the age of 18 he inaugurated
a new winter climbing Grade V in Douglas Gully of
Lochnagar ('having climbed well beyond the point
where we could safely withdraw and finding no belays
for an abseil we had little option but to continue
climbing'). By an odd chance, Patey's second,
Gordon Leslie, was nicknamed 'Goggs'—the name
of Raeburn's protesting second in the next-door gully
fifty years before.

As W H Murray comments:

*A phenomenal feature of this decade [the 1950s]
and the next was the output of new routes by Dr
Tom Patey; nothing like it, so long sustained in
such volume, and so widely spread, has been seen
before in the history of Scottish rock-climbing.*

A glance at the 1962 SMC *Cairngorms* guide confirms this: a random sortilege of twenty routes gives
Patey ten as first, or first winter, ascent. In 1956 on
the Mustagh Tower in the Karakorum, in an expedition including Joe Brown, he helped inaugurate the

lightweight, fast, dangerous and ethically satisfying 'Alpine' style of big-range climbing.

At the end of the 1950s he took up the post of GP to Ullapool, becoming the biggest doctor in Britain in terms of area covered. His phenomenal output of good new routes thereafter was in Wester Ross and Sutherland, even less likely to attract international celebrity than the Cairngorms.

He was killed in 1970, while abseiling down after the first ascent of a Sutherland sea-stack. The woolly jersey that he always wore may have become entangled with the karabiner and caused it to open.

Early man was assisted in his evolution by arms of the sea, glaciers and the like. These forced small populations to develop in imaginative ways on their own. In the same way, geography aided the climbers from Aberdeen. 'Unfortunately Braemar, the poor man's Courmayeur, is a difficult place to reach in mid-winter,' writes Patey with fake regret. 'The direct route from the south via the Devil's Elbow is often closed by deep snow for several months and the local Tigers still lack competition.'

Thus winter climbing separated into Aberdonians on Lochnagar, and the rest of world (and in particular the Creagh Dhu club of Glasgow) on Ben Nevis and in Glen Coe. The rest of the world accepted Vibrams —moulded rubber boot-soles—from 1947 and, as rubber won't grip on ice, the concomitant crampons. But Aberdonians preferred nails, on vegetated summer granite, and on ice that was interspersed with slime, right into the 1960s.

> *All snow conditions were regarded as climbing conditions. It merely became a question of adapting the technique to meet the prevailing conditions—névé, powder snow, verglassed rocks, frozen vegetation etc.*

Are you a piton person?

The piton, if used undiscriminatingly, could make climbing unnecessary. Thus in England, in the 1950s (and still today), the placing of a piton was the crime against—if not the Holy Ghost—at least the Spirit of Mountaineering. In belay-free granite, or on winter routes where one wanted actual protection as against an illusory ice-axe belay, it was necessary to abandon such strenuous ethics; and to take a position as delicate as anything on the snowy ledges of Carn Etchachan.

'Like the Queen of Spain's legs, a piton not only ought never to be seen, but must not be supposed even to exist.' (W H Murray on Lochnagar, 1939). J H B Bell treats it as a nasty foreign intrusion, writing it in italics. This also allows the *piton* ('I wish I could write it in a whisper') to spring from the page, so that the reader can assess just how frequently it was being deployed.

Or how infrequently. On a first ascent, one or at most two might be carried, to protect the crux and give a reasonable chance that failure might not be met with death. To give also, on occasion, a discreet handhold. Contrariwise, their non-use gave opportunities for sneering at climbers weaker or more sensible. Thus Patey, approaching Carn Etchachan:

> *The crackle of crisp snow underfoot, music to a hill lover's ears, was offset by the jangling of many pitons and karabiners—a recent assignment from the factories of Kincorth!*

He leads off up what was to become Scorpion, out of sight of Nicol, Grassick, and Mike Taylor trying a different line below.

> *They were engaged on a lusty rendering of bar-room ballads, punctuated by spells of hammering as they secured themselves against the leader's possible downfall. It reminded me of an absurd version of Verdi's 'Anvil Chorus'.*

The 1961 *Climbers' Guide*, the official word of the SMC, even advised one to protect the crux of Raeburn's 1907 route on the Shelter Stone Crag.

'The pioneer party was of the opinion that the climb was dangerous—it is so…' And yet the opening of gates in the ethical barrier did not lead to the fall of the city. Pitonage never threatened the integrity of Cairngorm climbing. And with the coming of alternative non-penetrative forms of protection, nuts and camming devices, the use of pitons became largely unnecessary.

The 1980s brought the straightening of the Devil's Elbow corner at the top of the Cairnwell; and even if it hadn't, it was time for the uniquely Aberdonian climbing style to hybridise back into, and invigorate, the main population.

John Cunningham, on Elephant Island with nothing to do, develops a technique with crampons and two hand-daggers for climbing vertical ice without step-cutting and indeed without an ice axe. (After the kick, the heel must be neither raised nor lowered, else you fall off.) Yvon Chouinard meets Cunningham at Glenmore Lodge below the northern corries of Cairn Gorm. Hamish MacInnes sees Chouinard's down-curved axe and develops the straight but inclined-head 'Terrordactyl'. Stab it in overhead and it doesn't pull back out; then hang from it on the wrist loops.

Combine crampons with two short ice axes with drop-down heads and you get the 'front-pointing' technique that makes ordinary vertical ice into a different and considerably easier game. Climbers move out onto the open faces, bare rock and frozen vegetation and shallow hoar-frost. They use the new axes on rock holds, twisted into cracks, stabbed into the frozen turf so abundant in the Cairngorms. A winter climb, on faces too steep to hold snow, is simply a rock climb in exceedingly uncomfortable conditions.

All feats of whatever kind are froth on the elixir distilled from rock and mountain. The froth too has its own respected place, being the elixir itself in one of its varied forms. Happy is the man who can drink deep.

Notes and references

W H Murray: *Mountaineering in Scotland* (1947).

J H B Bell: *A Progress in Mountaineering* (1950).

W H Murray: *Scotland's Mountains* (SMC 1987). A general guidebook including a history of mountaineering.

(p101) Goggs in a gully: SMCJ 1903. The gully is Raeburn's, on Lochnagar. Goggs presents himself as a reluctant 'Salvationist', the ancient term for a peakbagger, but went on to second Raeburn's Buttress on the Shelter Stone Crag.

Unattributed quotations are from Tom Patey, 'Cairngorm Commentary' (SMCJ 1963), 'Post War Winter Mountaineering' (Alpine Journal), and Etchachan Club Journal, all reprinted in *One Man's Mountains* (1971).

ROUTE 11 *Lairig an Lui to the Shelter Stone*

Start:	Linn of Dee
Distance to summit:	19.5km (12 miles)
Total ascent:	400m (1,400ft)

Take the following Route 12 from Derry Lodge along Glen Derry. Continue ahead through the pass and down past the gloomy Dubh Lochans, to the River Avon opposite the inhospitable Fords of Avon shelter. Take the rough path upstream to the left of River Avon and then of Loch Avon, to the Shelter Stone.

How good? Roundabout, rough and romantic.

11 Drovers

Robin [Rob Roy] was anes a weel-doing, pains-
taking drover, as ye wad see amang ten thousand.
It was a pleasure to see him in his belted plaid and
brogues, wi' his target [shield] at his back, and
claymore and dirk at his belt, following a hun-
dred Highland stots, and a dozen o' the gillies, as
rough and ragged as the beasts they drave.

Walter Scott: *Rob Roy*

Some of the earliest long-distance walkers went
treading in cowpats. Take a cattle-raider, turn him
through a right angle: instead of harrying livestock
from Aberdeenshire back to the wild West Highlands,
he's driving them south, towards the great cattle
markets at Crieff or Falkirk.

It's said that the Lairig an Laoigh, the Pass of the
Calves, is so named because it is gentler and has
better grazing than the shorter Lairig Ghru. This may
or may not be right: elsewhere in Scotland, 'Laoigh'
in Ben Lui or Liathach of Torridon refers to young
deer. But cattle gathered around Grantown did plod
south through the Lairig an Lui; while the Lairig
Ghru was an adventurous variant on the main drove

route from Sutherland and the far north-west.

Blar Dubh, at Beauly, was the gathering point of the Muir of Ord tryst. The name means 'Black Plain', appropriate for the trampled and smelly ground, with the cattle patiently steaming under the rain, peat-stained damp drovers bargaining with the local herdsmen, or snatching sleep in any dry corner. In later years, rough shacks stood as branches of the Bank of Scotland and the British Linen Bank; but for most of the two centuries of droving, the drover was his own bank, issuing promissory notes and a small amount of cash. According to sarcastic Sir Walter Scott, in his short story 'The Two Drovers', 'An oyster may be crossed in love… and a drover may be touched upon a point of honour.' But the trade could not have existed unless most of the drovers made honest payment. Suppose you wanted to send cash to Edinburgh: you'd give it to a drover. But then, sensibly, he'd leave the cash at home, or use it to buy cattle on the hoof; and pay your creditor at the other end with the proceeds of his cattle sale. Thus black cattle became a portable currency, the original 'cash cow'. Welsh drovers even founded one of the earliest Welsh banks, the Black Ox bank, with the ox himself on every bank note.

There were two roads south from Beauly. Those

who turned left would pass by Inverness and the Spey, with a further route choice at Aviemore. The standard line on southwards was down General Wade's military road, the present A9, through the Pass of Drumochter. But a drover late in the season would find that way well-trampled to black mud, its roadside grazing already chewed down, and might turn instead into the hills for the challenging passage of the Lairig Ghru.

A full day would see the herd through the stony passage of the Pools of Dee; but their ten to twelve miles wouldn't get them to the grassy flats at Chest of Dee. So we imagine them under Ben Macdui, choosing a patch of ground alongside the March Burn or the Tailors' Burn, not too stony, not too peaty, on the slopes crossed by the present path. Supper, shared with the drover's peat-blackened dog, was a brose of oatmeal from the drover's small sack; heated to porridge if the weather allowed a fire, otherwise cold, but possibly enriched with blood taken from the neck-vein of one of the stronger bullocks. Or better still, a lucky shot from a drover's fusee might bring down the stag roaring so mournfully on the slopes of Carn a' Mhaim. Bed was the heather, on the downwind side of a granite boulder, wrapped exactly as his reiving grandfather in tightly-woven woollen plaid. Dipping the plaid in the Dee would swell the fibres and render it waterproof.

Then at midnight to be roused, brush the frost from his shoulders, and take his turn at watching the cattle so they wouldn't wander in the moonlight and break ankles among the boulders.

At dawn, on down the Dee, driving the herd briskly between the shielings and enclosed lands at what's today White Bridge, then slowing to let them graze the headwaters of Tilt. Here the main drove road turned left, by way of Loch Loch, to cross the Highland Line at Kirkmichael.

From the great cattle sales at Crieff or, later, Falkirk, the herds continued south, dividing around the Ochils, then through the passes of the Cheviots into England. After fattening on the green fields of Yorkshire or East Anglia, they plodded onwards to London, to become salt beef for the Navy or to feed the industrial revolution. By the 1850s, 100,000 cattle a year were walking the length of the UK to the slaughterhouses of Smithfield. In 1859, Queen Victoria on her way up Ben Macdui found Glen Derry all torn up by the hooves of the drove, but by then the trade was in decline. As agriculture improved, or landowners developed their ground for sheep or deer, land alongside the drove road was enclosed, cutting off the essential fuel supply for cattle on the move. The new-built turnpike roads imposed tolls. Worse, their hard surfaces damaged the feet of the cattle. Special iron shoes were developed, like miniature horseshoes but divided two to a foot for the separated hoof. The half-wild cattle did not, however, stand patiently as horses would. Shoeing was a matter of roping them and turning them upside down on their backs; and this might have to happen several times along the way.

In 1981, an intrepid group of orange Highland cattle set out from Skye to retrace the steps of their ancestors to Crieff Mart. They weren't terribly good at it. They suffered from sore feet all the way (though that could be blamed on our tarred roads), they fell into rivers, and they proved quite incapable of swimming the straights at Kylerhea.

The selection pressure of constantly being stolen and harried across rough country in the dark: this rendered the black cattle of the clans small, agile, and light on their feet. From them have descended the orange, bendy-horned, shaggy Highland breed of today, so fond of standing ankle-deep in lochs in front of well-known mountain scenes. Two hundred years when the lean and fit have got killed and eaten while the beefy and indolent get to breed and reproduce: this has been enough to lose the Highland cow her fine mountain edge.

Mountaineering humans are not normally castrated or slaughtered for the pot, so we may be losing our hunter-gatherer adaptations slightly slower than that. But we must wonder how much of our hill skill, since the Stone Age, has been simply bred out of us? A bothy lifestyle, peat-scented breeks, and a borrowed cow brought back from Angus—these do not in today's world lead to financial, social or sexual success. So gratitude is due to the manufacturers of outdoor Gore-tex gear, doing their very best to restore glamour to the game of plodding, mud-stained, through the Lairig an Lui.

Notes and references

A R B Haldane: *The Drove Roads of Scotland* (1952) is the definitive history.

Walter Scott: 'The Two Drovers', plus introduction to *Rob Roy*.

(p117) The drove of 1981: *The Famous Highland Drove Walk* by Irvine Butterfield (1996).

ROUTE 12 Coire Etchachan

Start:	Linn of Dee
Distance to summit:	16.5km (10½ miles)
Total ascent:	950m (3,100ft)

Path leads out of the car park—cyclists must take the track 1km to the east. Broad boring track leads to Derry Lodge. Cross a footbridge to take path west of River Derry, recrossing to join the former track now reduced to path status. After 3km, fork left into Coire Etchachan, past the small bothy, and up to the outflow of Loch Etchachan. Path leads up left, eventually alongside tops of crags of Coire Sputan Dearg, but vanishes at the plateau. Head west to the summit.

In descent: Don't turn north-east too soon. Head carefully east from the summit to crag tops and only then turn down left, with the path soon forming.

How good? Scenically varied and interesting. Technically easy, on tracks and well-built paths—Queen Victoria did most of it without dismounting. I like this one as a descent because of its kindly gradients. Many shorten the 5km to Derry Lodge, that Victoria drove in her carriage, by biking it.

12 Victoria Walks

Never shall I forget this day or the impression this very grand scene made upon me; truly sublime and impressive; such solitude.

Queen Victoria: *Leaves from the Journal of Our Life in the Highlands (1859)*

What it was that possessed the British monarchy to indulge with such enthusiasm, expense, and unself-consciousness in the creation of a neo-feudal fairyland in the mountains ... seemed to me a point worthy of examination. ... Despite the misfortune of her birth, Vicci was—put charitably—the best of her bunch, and I'm sure she would have made a half-decent bothy companion.

Ian R Mitchell: *On the Trail of Queen Victoria in the Highlands (2000)*

It was raining on the Macdui plateau. Rainwater dripped steadily off the projecting stones of the surveyors' cairn; rain blackened the western wall of the surveyors' hut. The few tussocks of moss campion lay flat on the gravel, their leaves weighed down with raindrops, their flowers long gone. Hungry and cold, the great grey primate plodded across the rocks, hoping for the flicker of a ptarmigan's tail behind a boulder. He vanished downhill into the mist, leaving a perfect set of footprints across the summer's last, late-lying snowfield at the top of Garbh Uisge.

The prints filled up with water, softened at their edges, and dissolved into the snowbank. The afternoon started to pass. The Tailors' Burn, lively with fresh rain, tinkled endlessly into the grey cloud-hole that was the Lairig Ghru. After a while, it stopped raining.

Downslope, in the direction of the Etchachan, came the sound of moving stones. Then the low murmur of male voices, the rasp of a nailed boot, the clash of hooves on stone. Shapes in the mist resolved into human figures walking, a person plaid-wrapped on a walking pony, more ponies behind. At the edge of the summit boulderfield the ponies halted, and there was talk between the mounted few and the kilted walkers below. The mounted dismounted, there was yet more talk, and then all started across the boulders with small shrieks of excitement. The two youngest made their way ahead, peered into the ruined hut, touched the cairn, and ran on to peer into the clouded depths of the Lairig. The kilted servants unhitched the pony-panniers, lugged them up the final slope, and started to unfold plaids and deploy hampers alongside the wall of the hut. The short and somewhat dumpy woman made her way carefully across the stones, ignoring offered elbows from companions and servants. She stopped occasionally, peering at the nearby mist and boulders with half-raised eyebrows, as if pleased to see that it was all behaving itself appropriately… and, several minutes after her offspring, made it to the cairn.

It was 7th October 1859. Queen Victoria had bagged her fourth Munro.

Grant was just feeding the queen's pony (also called Victoria), John Brown was probably hunting down the number-two whisky bottle, when the sun came out. Through rainwashed air there was a view that included all three of Her Majesty's previous Munros (Carn a' Chlamain, Carn a' Choire Bhoidheach, and Lochnagar). The summit boulders steamed, and even the flattened humps of moss campion perked up a little. The last grey cloud dissolved in the Lairig Ghru, so they got to see the Dee and the trampled black path of the cattle-drovers. There was whisky, and smoked ham, and oatcakes. Brown stretched out with telescope at the plateau edge to spy for deer, with kilt decorously tucked lest the breeze lift the tweed and display the figure-hugging tartan shorts, final line of defence between the queenly gaze and his bare bum. The Prince Regent found a smoky-brown Cairngorm crystal, just right to be bound in silver so as to make some lucky princess or queen a really ugly locket or brooch. The young princess fell over and scraped her shin but it didn't bleed.

Everybody had the most tremendous fun.

On the way down, the Queen actually stopped and told the most helpful of her servants just what fun it all was. This was not a normal social situation. Even so, John Brown, somewhat awkwardly, managed to convey that he was having fun as well. 'It's very pleasant to walk with a person [Prince Albert] who is always "content".'

Down over the stones of Coire Etchachan the going was too stony for riding and the ponies had to be led. Prince Albert took a potshot at a ptarmigan. The report echoed off the damp granite overhead, and two more ptarmigan came up in a flicker of white wings. As usual, His Royal Highness had missed his bird. Down in Glen Derry, Victoria Queen of England climbed back onto Victoria the pony. The fording of the river required more excited shrieks and the queen got her feet wet. But Albert and Brown weren't allowed to make a fuss about that, as she was concentrating on enjoying the noble pine trees.

Under those noble pines the shadows were gathering as they reached the carriages at Luibeg shielings.

The royal party passed their plaids up to Brown and Grant riding out in the breeze on top. As they crossed the new stone bridge over the Linn of Dee, the low sun streamed under the pinetops and across the inside of the carriage. They turned east for Balmoral, and the interior darkened. The Queen closed her eyes and started turning over telling phrases for *Leaves from the Journal of Our Life in the Highlands*. The fading sunlight: didn't it just resemble the purplish bloom on a plum? But come to think of it, she'd used the bloom on the plum twice already. 'A sublime and solemn effect, so wild, so solitary…'? Now, that was going to get them.

They reached the castle at 8.00. Behind the stables, the bagpiper was tuning up for supper time. The Queen climbed out, slightly stiff. Muttering under her breath ('grandest, wildest scenery imaginable… magnificent wild rocks, precipices, corries…') she made her way in to tea.

Seventeen miles away, and three thousand feet above, the last mauve sunlight was leaving the cairn of Ben Macdui. Like an early shadow the Grey Man moved silently across the boulders, widely skirting the dangerous-smelling piles of poo from Victoria the pony... and crouched suddenly, to lick off the boulders a smear of duck-liver paté.

The fun they had

Queen Victoria, ruling all that she surveyed at the age of eighteen without any elderly family members to tell her how, was in the interesting situation of being able to invent her own lifestyle. In theory, she could have come up with ice-climbing, Tupperware parties, or a new and more enticing form of orgy.

In the event, she selected from what was already around. So, from the English aristocracy she and Albert imported horse-riding and a love of killing things with guns, Albert's cheerful incompetence being in the grand tradition of English amateurism. From the middle classes came a love of respectability, plus the ability to take pleasure in activities only very mildly enjoyable. (Earlier accounts have given her too little credit for the intensely-applied Englishness with which she managed to appreciate bagpipe music during breakfast.) From Sir Walter Scott she took the ethos of Highland kitsch, removed from it all the exciting bits, and then managed to extract plenty of excitement anyway. From Albert's Thuringerwald she imported Christmas trees and long-distance mountain outings. From the folk-tradition of Deeside she stole the Highland Games, subverting it into a genteel, bourgeois, but only slightly boring entertainment. And also from Deeside tradition she took a certain social attitude.

Queen V has been described as a crypto-democrat. This is a mistake. She did not believe that she and a Deeside peasant or Ballater shopkeeper could talk on terms of equality. But she did believe that they could talk. Fifty years before Victoria hit Deeside, Lady Elizabeth Grant had hobnobbed with drovers, tenants and timbermen at the Ballater Tryst, and recorded her sadness at the passing of this backchat between the classes. Victoria, to the scandal of her aristocracy, revived this social intercourse. In footnotes to her diary she fails to record the lineage of Prince Wurtenburg of Holstein Bolstein—instead devoting half a page to the family and antecedents of Ross the Piper and John Brown. And it was this in particular that delighted her middle-class subjects while affronting her own family: the Prince of Wales expressing his 'indignation and *disgust* at the Queen publishing her Journal!!!' After her death, they banished the statue of John Brown to a wooded thicket well away from the castle—but it's on the Balmoral Blue Trail of today, and his pedestal is a tall one so you can look under his kilt and see the tartan trews as rendered in bronze.

Ian Mitchell, Marxist and entertaining describer of Victoria's Highland adventures, thinks that in the conversation on Ben Macdui, Brown was simply laying on the flattery. But on other occasions, when she'd done something stupid with a stirrup, he would address his monarch as 'Wumman!': this is scarcely sycophantic. And I read their exchange just as two not-especially-sophisticated Munro-baggers enjoying a nice day on Ben Macdui.

Queen Victoria's longest expedition was a two-day circuit of the Cairngorms, by Glen Feshie, the Spey, and Tomintoul. She masqueraded as 'Lady Churchill', and there were great giggles when Grant the ghillie slipped up and addressed Prince Albert as 'Your Royal Highness'. She bagged in all nine Munros, which is more than almost anyone else alive at the time, and probably more than any other member of the Royal Family ever. (Bonnie Prince Charlie got four, including Sgurr Thuilm at Glenfinnan. The Duke of Edinburgh goes up Broad Cairn by Landrover. Possibly the present Prince Charles has outdone his great-great-granny.) She certainly invented pony-trekking, as well as the bourgeois monarchy. But she should also be credited with a large part in our mild and respectable pursuit of simply plodding up hills, in Scotland, in the rain.

Notes and references

Leaves from the Journal of Our Life in the Highlands by Queen Victoria (ed. Arthur Helps). The first edition of 1868 is available cheaply on Abebooks, or pay about £20 for the attractively illustrated edition from the Folio Society (ISBN: 0850670705, 1973).

(p126) 'Indignation and disgust!!!'—reported by the Duke of Cambridge and recorded in the diary of his wife's lady-in-waiting, Lady Geraldine Somerset; from Introduction to the 1973 Folio Society edition of *Leaves*.

(p127) On the Trail of Queen Victoria in the Highlands by Ian R Mitchell (Luath Press 2000 ISBN 0 946487 79 0) credits 'Vicci' with eight Munros, but I've persuaded the author that she passed the summit of a ninth, Carn a' Choire Bhoidheach, close enough to count.

ROUTE 13 *Derry Cairngorm*

Start:	Linn of Dee
Distance to summit:	14km (9 miles)
Total ascent:	1,200m (3,700ft)

Follow Route 12 to Derry Lodge, cross the footbridge there, and head straight up the spur opposite on a faint path. A first rocky hump is approached from the right, then the path skirts the steep top rim of Coire na Saobhaidh—it's quite exposed, so if windy or icy, divert over the summit of Carn Crom.

Head north on intermittent path to bouldery Derry Cairngorm, then north-west across a bouldery col. Skirt the west flank of Creagan a' Choire Etchachan to the path across its back, Route 12 again.

How good? Rugged but with good views, and you bag the bonus Munro of Derry Cairngorm.

13 High Hats

'Going to Macdui?' asks my father: 'Look out for my wristwatch, would you? In fact, look out for two of them.'

In the event, when we got there, there was a smell of high-octane fuel right down to the col of Carn a' Mhaim. And up on the plateau, helicopters were carrying away polluted snow from the aeroplane crash of a couple of months earlier. All the summit ground of Ben Macdui had been gone over with metal detectors. And the forty-year old remains of my Dad's wristwatches had surely now been detected, tagged, and carried away to the United States.

To lose one wristwatch on Ben Macdui is bad. To lose two could be called careless. The things are strapped on, after all. What one usually loses—and finds—are hats.

In TGO (The Great Outdoors) magazine of October 2003, Chris Townsend suggested that it doesn't much matter what hat you buy. That struck me as a pretty provocative statement. A hat for the hill—is that really something you go into a shop and *buy*? Over the years I've acquired so many hats it's hard to give each of them a fair airing. But only one of them came from the High Street: the acrylic stocking-cap with the emblem of

Ben Macdui across Loch Etchachan

Manchester United. I picked that one up, not actually in the high street's shops, but in the gutter as I cycled along, and it goes nicely with my red Keela waterproof.

The other four came off the hill. And as well as having my head in, they also hold my memories.

There's the Great Outdoor Challenge hat, plucked off a certain greyly granite Munro during a coast to coast walk in 2001. It's a stylish hat with a logo, although I usually wear it inside-out so as not to be too trendy. If its previous inhabitant wants to resume occupancy, just write and say which Munro summit it fell off on.

Then there's the Lakeland bothy hat. That's a wide-brimmed exploratory sort of headpiece, good for fetching water in. I wore that one day and night through the Picos de Europa, and bought it a little Picos badge for its hatband afterwards. And there's the floppy sunhat from Ben Nevis. I picked that one up, quite literally for nothing, at the end of a long day running over old snowfields along the Grey Corries.

Handiest hat of all was a tiny acrylic number that came off Carlin's Cairn in Galloway. Once green, long exposure had turned the upper side a sort of heathery mauve: excellent camouflage for bivvying out in grouse country. I shared several hill years with that hat, and then it left me on Nine Standards Rigg—the western slope of it, heading down to Kirkby Stephen.

Which leads to the question: do hats have their own agenda? As they wander from head to head around the world's upland areas, are some of them simple ramblers, while others vie for the title of Top Hat by bagging ever more summits, more human occupants? Perhaps some scented tweedy bonnet, a forgotten trout-fly in the brim, moved from Robertson to Naismith and bagged the Munros before any human occupant. My faded acrylic may now have lain lost on more different hills than even I have myself…

From time to time a hat must finally die: shrivelled

in a hot wash, cremated in a bothy fire, trampled irretrievably into the peat of the Cheviot, though we know from Tilley's advertising that a good hat keeps going even after being passed three times through an elephant. And occasionally some cold-headed but warm-hearted hillwalker has gone into Tiso's or George Fisher, handed over actual money, and launched a new headpiece into the hat community.

There are the practicalities of the hat. It's got to be small enough to stuff in a pocket—hat off then on again is simpler than rummaging for an extra base layer. At the same time it's got to be big enough to pillow you, whichever way up you lay your head, when in your sleeping bag on the stony summit of Derry Cairngorm. But these are trivial considerations.

A hat is an emotional amplifier. Heavy boots can increase the load on your back by up to five kilograms, but a light-hearted titfer will counteract all that. More than half of hillwalking takes place in the head; and where is the head but inside that timeless classic, the much-loved woolly bobble? Somewhere in the Lairig Ghru under Lurcher's Crag, preserved in the peat, is a hat of blind hillwalker Syd Scroggie's, dropped in 1958:

Padded, peaked, buckled and capable of being let down over the ears in severe weather, it was called

my Afrika Korps hat from its resemblance to the
headgear worn by those blond giants under the
command of Rommel.

It's nice to be on Ben Macdui on a misty autumn morning, or at Ettrick Head on a snowy Ne'erday. But how much better to be there underneath some original and appropriate headwear. For Ben Macdui, surely, the scratchy all-wool Balaclava. For the Ettricks, the simplicity of your classic cotton baseball cap. At Esk Hause on a crisp January afternoon, who is making the most of the penetrating winter light: the man, bare-headed, or his friend in her mauve and scarlet Peruvian bonnet, clashing so vigorously with her orange fleece?

Whether it's Victoria's broad-brimmed thing with feathers at Linn of Dee, or the Basque handkerchief in the Pyrenees, the simple banana leaf on Kilimanjaro or the bright orange balaclava against December blue on Ben Macdui, the hat is where it's at.

I strode down Glen Derry, without either of my father's watches, still wearing the simple black acrylic headwear I set out in. But in the car-park, just beside my car, a pair of slim green-and-gold trekking poles was leaning against a tree, waiting for me their new owner to take them on the next stage of their life's trek.

ROUTE 14 *Lochan Uaine of Derry Cairngorm*

Start:	Linn of Dee
Distance to summit:	17km (10½ miles)
Total ascent:	1,100m (3,900ft)

Follow Route 12 into Glen Derry, staying on the track now downgraded to path for 2km to pass through a fenced enclosure for regenerating pines. Fork off left, cross the river (which can be problematic) and head steeply up into Coire an Lochain Uaine.

Pass around the lochan, and zigzag up steep broken ground to the right of a waterfall to reach the plateau. Turn left to reach Derry Cairngorm by a grassy gangway among the boulders.

How good? A rough route, whose reward is the least-visited of the Cairngorms' four Lochans Uaine.

14 Granite

He had become transformed into a grim realist.
He would talk about nothing but granite!

H V Morton (Beachcomber) in Dalbeattie:
In Scotland Again (1933)

According to philosopher Henri Poincaré, 'If God speaks to man, he undoubtedly uses the language of mathematics.' But when His word materialised itself as Ben Macdui, the language he used was granite.

That language is limited. Granite speaks in damp slabs that gleam with slime and algae under the stray sunbeam. Granite conveys its inner self in dark heather and black mud. Here are no airy ridges, but glacier-scraped summits dotted with round boulders. The crags are big and forbidding, but hidden in shadowed corries that you reach through a lot of bog and an awkward river crossing.

And then, as a light-hearted moment, granite offers a tor. But nobody's laughing.

Elsewhere in the world, we find granite in its youthful grace and vigour. The Tatras of Poland and Slovenia show granite in playful childhood, leaping into the sky with happy shouts, dressing itself up in twisted 'elbow-wood' of dwarf pine, and bright wildflowers. Granite is adolescent in Yosemite, expressing itself in fantastic huge half-dome and sheer precipice; ignore the attention-seeking gestures and golly, what a sulk! Granite adult is Mont Blanc, armed in ice, self-confident and handsome. But here in Britain, we have granite in maturity, and granite in old age.

On Dartmoor, after an hour of moorland in the mist, and knee-deep streams to wash away the stains of knee-deep bogs, come upon a tor and wander round and round its rugged rocks trying to make them adopt some intelligible shape.

On Arran, or the Mountains of Mourne, enjoy granite whose steep slopes are boulders with holes between, all hidden under heather. But oh, the cones of them: each tall triangle topped off with its nipple of bare granite. Between the brown bits is the piercing blue of the Silent Valley Reservoir, or else, between A' Chir and Goatfell, the greenish sea. And at lunchtime, granite sharpens the savour of the spring water, granite is rough under the bum.

In the Galloway hills, coarse yellow grasses alternate with grey slab, which you walk as on a city pavement, avoiding the occasional street furniture supplied by glacier-deposited boulders. The Devil plays at bowls with these boulders on the plateau of Craignaw. He plays at bowls again on the hills that lie south of Glen Coe stretching away to Ben Cruachan; also among the hills of Wicklow.

But when we look at the Seven Ages of Granite, it's the Cairngorms that wear the long white beard, that carry the grandeur and tragedy of King Lear.

From Derry Cairngorm around to Loch Etchachan, it's boulders, bleakness, bare granite and old snow. Grey boulders lie in rows and heaps around the area's smallest Lochan Uaine. Alongside the waterfall rise slabs of speckled granite, shining with the dampness that's on them. Sun breaks through, the sky is eggshell blue, the high slabs shine to dazzle, and the lochan goes green to match its name.

Aig Allt an Lochain Uaine,
Bha mi uair 'tamh,
Ged bha 'n t-aite fuar
Bha 'n fhardach fuasach blath,
Ged thigeadh gaoth 'o thuath orm
'Us cathadh luath o'n aird
Bha Allt an Lochain Uaine
Le 'fhuaim ga m'chuir gu pramh.

At stream of Lochan Uaine
was sheltering from the storm;
though cold it was, the corrie,
my lodging cosy warm
Though come the north wind on me
and snowdrift quick and deep
the Stream of Lochan Uaine
with noise put me to sleep

William Smith, known as Rynuie after his holding Ruighe Naoimhe, served under Sir John Moore in the Peninsular War. In later life he worked as both poet and poacher. His gun had been presented to him by his own Laird of Rothiemurchus, presumably on the understanding that he would be using it on the rival Mar Lodge Estate. His poaching bothy at Lochan Uaine gave him a good view of gamekeepers approaching up Glen Derry. His song about it was an Aberdeenshire anthem in the years when the Gaelic was still spoken. As already described in Chapter 5, his descendant Carrie Mackenzie of Whitewell took to hanging about even higher up on Ben Macdui. And she believed that Rynuie was up there with her, in spirit at least, patrolling the granite as the Great Grey Man of Macdui.

Melt together milk, butter and sugar in a saucepan. Let it solidify slowly and you get fudge. Cool it quick and the result is toffee: same ingredients, but a totally different feel between the teeth. The difference is due to crystallisation. Cool it quickly so that crystals don't have a chance to form, and the result is a super-cooled liquid, or glass. Toffee, and basalt lava, are both examples of glass. Thus the toffee-formed windows of the witch's little house in the woods, like the glass ones of ancient cathedrals, will slowly flow down to thicken the bottom part of the pane.

As rocks go, granite is not a toffee but a fudge. Granite is formed from upwelling molten magma that didn't make it all the way up into the open air, but came to a stop still six kilometres underground. At that depth, heat can escape only over thousands of years. So granite has big crystals, big enough to see. Its name comes from the Latin *granum*, meaning a grain.

The ingredients of fudge are sugar, butter and milk. The ingredients of granite are quartz, biotite mica and feldspar. Other ingredients add colour and flavour—vanilla, dark olivine rocks, cochineal and so on.

Quartz is hard and angular; usually white, but always with a shine. Biotite supplies the black or brown speckles. Feldspar comes in either whitish-

Waterfall at Lochan Uaine

pink or pinkish-white: sodium feldspar is pale grey, but potassium feldspar is pink or red. Some slow stirring in the earth's mantle 200 million years ago gave Macdui the pale grey sort, while the foot of Loch Avon three miles away got the marginally more cheerful pink.

Feldspar is softer and rots, and this determines the whole geography of granite. Ordinary rainwater, given long enough, can wash the feldspar away. And so the sharp edges of granite get dissolved off, and granite boulders are round. But quartz is hard: its supercooled, non-crystalline form is window glass. Thus weathered granite is rough from the projecting quartz. And granite gives good grip for the feet, but offers few sharp edges for handholds. The joints in granite weather open, to give round-edged cracks and chimneys.

As granite weathers, the quartz crystals fall to the ground as sharp-edged gravel. The gravel drains well, and gives plateau ground that's good to walk on. But it forms only a thin mat of vegetation, and this is easily broken by feet or streams. If the ground is at all steep, the loose gravel below is soon washed out, and path erosion follows. The most popular paths up Macdui are relatively gentle, or else on boulders and bare rock. But Queen Victoria's route up Coire Etchachan was grass on gravel, and is now, accordingly, a renovated stone stepway. The team that restored it in 2000 trained on the steeper, busier, and much worse-eroded granite of Goatfell.

What makes granite granite, then, is the fundamental physics of fudge. The Big Rock Candy Mountain (where good hobos go after they die) would erode rather rapidly under ordinary rain—but 'there ain't no rain and there ain't no snow' and instead pure alcohol trickles down the rocks in little streams to form lakes of whisky and of gin. The butter and water out of fudge are soluble in alcohol, the sugar crystals less so. And the Big Rock Candy Mountain may have a landscape not unlike the Cairngorms, with the cigarette trees struggling for rootholds in the sugar-candy gravel.

Is rock candy good to climb on? According to those who should know, it has a month's-worth of routes on it and is the 'Colorado equivalent of the Apron in Yosemite'. Sadly, though, the BRCM of the Platte River is actually made of sandstone. And the song-world Rock Candy, with its arcane and sticky-fingered climbing style, is a tougher walk-in than even big Ben Macdui. At least, according to the original last lines of the ballad:

I've hiked and hiked till my feet are sore
And I'll be damned if I hike any more
To be buggered sore like a hobo's whore
In the Big Rock Candy Mountains.

Notes and references

The 'seven ages of granite' above is fanciful. In fact the granites of the Cairngorms and Galloway date from the Caledonian Orogeny (Scotland crunches into England) 400 million years ago. The Tatras and Mont Blanc granites were emplaced during the Hercynian Orogeny ('Africa Crunch') 250 million years ago, which makes their rocks the same age as Dartmoor's, but they owe their exciting shapes to the sudden uplift and erosion during the rise of the Alps which started 50 million years ago and is still going on. Yosemite granite (the 'Sierra Nevada batholith') is from the Cretaceous, about 100 million years ago, generated above the subduction zone where the Pacific slides in under North America. Arran and Mourne are recent arrivals, formed during the opening of the Atlantic 50 million years ago. All the hills owe their shapes of today to the current Ice Age.

(p139) William Rynuie: CCJ I p329 and III p19, quoted in the 1938 SMC *Cairngorms* area guide; also in Affleck Gray(see chapter 16 below).

In Rynuie's verse, hillgoers can click in to 'fuar', 'gaoth', and 'tuath', (cold, wind, north) all elements of hill names. 'Prath' is a sleeping spell. 'Luath', quick, was the name of Robert Burns' collie dog. 'Aird' is a projection or promontory. My translation is fairly literal.

ROUTE 15 *Sron Riach*

Start:	Linn of Dee
Distance to summit:	14km *(8½ miles)*
Total ascent:	950m (3,200ft)

Follow Route 12 to cross the footbridge just north of Derry Lodge. Turn left, along the north side of Luibeg Burn, over meadows, then a good path. After 2km fork right up Glen Luibeg on a path that gradually vanishes. Go straight up the spur, past a couple of small tors, to reach Sron Riach. A well-defined ridge and then a steeper spur lead to the plateau south of Macdui summit.

How good? A pleasant route, but you don't gather either of the outlying Munros.

15 The Cause of Tors

Once you've seen it, the ice is obvious. It explains why corries like Coire Etchachan have steep-carved head walls, and face north or east but hardly ever south-west. It explains why U-shaped valleys such as upper Glen Avon, where they level off, have a hollow that holds a loch like Loch Avon. Stand on the slabs above that loch's head and it's hard not to see the ice sliding over and smoothing them. It explains the odd rocks known as 'erratics', perched on ridge tops and sometimes of schist, where what's underneath is granite.

But until you've seen it, it isn't obvious at all. 'Could scratches and polish just be due to *ice*?' asked Roderick Impey Murchison, a top geologist who invented the entire Silurian and Permian periods (a total of 75 million years) and was awarded a diamond-encrusted snuffbox by the Tsar of Russia, but still got rather a lot of geology quite wrong. William Hopkins of Cambridge pointed out that ice transporting boulders is an 'obvious mechanical absurdity'. In 1841 the Geological Society of Edinburgh admitted that there might be some general merit in the theory but that it obviously didn't apply to Scotland.

Hopkins and the Edinburgh Geological Society

can themselves be seen as moral fossils, preserving ancient attitudes in rock-solid minds. A short journey to the coffee shop would have let them inspect the sketchbooks of some of the thousands of English tourists who, since the end of the Napoleonic Wars, had been to Chamonix to prance about among the glacier boulders on the Mer de Glace.

Tors for thought

But is it not completely natural that large rocks should lie around on the mountain landscape? Not at all, says the reader. The rocks are obviously odd, they certainly should have spotted it.

OK, cleverclogs reader. So how many times have you walked past the rock tors on the way up Sron Riach, or across the tops of Beinn Mheadhoin and Ben Avon? You're not Roderick Murchison and you know all about the Ice Age and how it only ended 13,000 years ago. Did the Ice Age flow right over the top without knocking these rocks over? Or did the Cairngorm Tors somehow form themselves in the brief millennia since the Ice Ages? The Barns of Bynack, were they transported perhaps by Fingalian giants, or was it all down to Noah's Flood…?

The tors might have formed since the end of the Ice Age, or the Ice Age didn't cover them, or else they have somehow survived underneath the ice-cap. These are the three answers, and all three are hard to believe.

There is a mechanism for uncovering rocks in the brief but chilly millennia since the end of the ice. It's called gelifluction, a creeping of thawed soil downhill over a layer of permafrost. However: the tors are on the tops. There would be little downhill creeping of the soil on the summit of Beinn Mheadhoin, because the place is flat. Furthermore: at the Argyll Stone in particular, glacial erratics, loose stones dropped off by the melting glacier, are still lying around on the ground. So that soil hasn't crept away downhill. (The Argyll Stone is the small tor above, and three kilometres south of, Loch an Eilein, at NH904040.)

So was the upper Cairngorm surface ice-free? Unlikely, given the present-day climate, the evident vigour of glaciers in the Lairig Ghru, and those erratics around the Argyll Stone. Mapping of erratic boulders over the rest of Scotland suggests a Cairngorm ice-cap that was 500 metres deep even over the summits.

In fact, today's theories, so much more plausible than Noah and his flood, have the tors forming, underground, fifty million years ago during the Tertiary era. At that time Scotland was warm, wet, and somewhere in what's now northern France.

Groundwater juiced up by rotting plant life trickled

down the joints of the granite and attacked the susceptible feldspar; and the granite just rotted away. Here and there, where the granite was more compact, cores that the rain didn't reach are buried future tors. The rotten granite and quartz gravel were washed away by flash floods, or blown away by desert winds; soil creep, as described above, finished off the job.

Accordingly, we must conclude that the tors survived underneath 500 metres of ice. Leaving aside that it's obviously impossible, there are some evidences. The tors of Dartmoor, never iced, are even more tottery and balanced than the Cairngorm ones. Some Cairngorm tors do seem wonky, as having been pushed downhill. Stob Bac an Fhurain, on Ben Avon,

Sron Riach

has had its top lifted off and dropped alongside.

Glaciologists today distinguish between ice with a thin layer of underlying water, and ice that's frozen to the ground. Ice that is on flatter surfaces, or higher up and so colder, tends to stay frozen down. Once the ice is on the move it generates friction heat; this adds more underlying water, and speeds up the slide. The now galloping glacier scrapes out a glacial valley. Snow blows in, thickening the ice and further increasing its downhill slide and its gouge power.

The Cairngorms had both lively-slidey ice, over what became the Lairig Ghru and Loch Avon, and stuck-down ice, across the tops. On those upper layers, ice sheared from the ground up rather than flowing as a whole: it deformed gradually, without knocking down the delicate rock-structures underneath.

Across the plateau, stuck-down ice has preserved pre-existing scenes of shallow valleys and gentle streams, drearily reminiscent of Dartmoor. Slidey ice gives us the sudden surprise as we reach the rim of Coire Sputan Dearg. It takes granite, yes: but also two kinds of ice to make the Cairngorms.

Notes

The tor conundrum was posed in SMCJ 1983.
Answers on www.fettes.com/Cairngorms/tors.htm

ROUTE 16 Carn a' Mhaim

Start:	Linn of Dee
Distance to summit:	15km (9½ miles)
Total ascent:	1,200m (4,100ft)

Follow Route 12 to cross the footbridge just north of Derry Lodge. Turn left, to the right of Luibeg Burn; after 2km fork down left to the bouldery ford of Luibeg Burn—there is a footbridge 400 metres upstream. Path leads on around the flank of Carn a' Mhaim. From the path's highest point head up the steep south-east spur to Carn a' Mhaim.

Follow the broad, pathed ridge-line down north-west for 2km, and ascend the flank of Ben Macdui by a gruelling slope of steep boulders. At the plateau turn north-west across the top of the Tailors' Burn to the summit.

How good? In the Cairngorms, this is the best, indeed only, ridge walk. But the final climb is tough.

16 The Collector of Jade and the Grey Man

... and when the deed was done
I heard among the solitary hills
Low breathings coming after me, and sounds
Of undistinguishable motion, steps
Almost as silent as the turf they trod.

Wordsworth: *The Prelude* Book I. Aged nine, he is stealing
woodcock from other poachers' snares by night.

Ben Macdui does not take its name from the Great
Grey Man of Ben Macdui—it works the other way
round. But Sgurr Thormaid on Skye does take its
name from Professor Norman Collie (1859–1942):
Tormaid is the Gaelic way of saying Norman.

Collie also gave his name to a pinnacle on Bidean
nam Bian, a carved footstep in Moss Gill on Scafell,
the less difficult way to get up the Bhasteir Tooth, and
the unexpected ledge, high above the Cuillin's Coire
Lagan, that leads you around the side of Sgurr Mhic
Choinnich. He did not, however, invent the leggy
black-and-white dog that likes to bite hillrunners.

English, but with Scots ancestors, Collie was a
Professor of Chemistry at Glasgow University and
a Fellow of the Royal Society. He's credited as the

discoverer of the element neon, inventor of the neon lamp, and the first medical user of X-ray photography. He was Vice-President of the Royal Geographical Society, President of both the Alpine Club and the Cairngorm Club. He was a collector of Chinese jade and a lover of the Cairngorms.

The sculptured sides of Braeriach, seen from Sgoran Dubh Mor, are in reality far richer in beautiful, intricate mountain sculpture than the whole face of the Matterhorn, as seen from the Riffel Alp.

The story goes: at the dinner of the Cairngorm Club in December 1925, Professor Collie, almost despite himself, admits to a strange experience on Ben Macdui in 1891.

I was returning from the cairn on the summit in a mist when I began to think I heard something else than merely the noise of my own footsteps. For every few steps I took I heard a crunch, and then another crunch as if someone was walking after me but taking steps three or four times the length of my own.

I said to myself, 'This is all nonsense.' I listened and heard it again but could see nothing in the mist. As I walked on and the eerie crunch, crunch, sounded behind me I was seized with terror and took to my heels, staggering blindly among the boulders for four or five miles nearly down to Rothiemurchus Forest.

Whatever you make of it I do not know, but there is something very queer about the top of Ben MacDhui and I will not go back there again by myself I know.

Others then admitted to hearing footsteps, seeing a giant figure, or experiencing terror seizures. A Deeside legend was tracked down that

a big spectral figure has been seen at various times during the last five years walking about on the tops of the Cairngorms. Moreover, it has got a name—'Ferlie More', to wit.

The Gaelic Fear Liath Mor means Great Grey Man. Here are one or two of his juicier sightings.

Ernest A Baker, in *The Highlands with Rope and Rucksack* published the year before Collie's talk, described 'an eerie feeling on Macdui, such that he would not willingly return to the mountain'.

A second mountaineering academic, Dr Alexander Kellas (1868–1921), actually saw the creature, which Collie didn't. Kellas, a Chemistry lecturer at Middlesex Hospital Medical School, achieved notable climbs in Sikkim (now part of China) including the first ascent, in 1911, of Pauhunri (7,128 metres). He recounted his Macdui experience to Collie in about 1910. He died, four years before Collie's after-dinner speech, on the first Everest expedition of 1921, the one in which Mallory and Raeburn also took part.

Kellas did not record his experience, and all accounts are second-hand. He was with his brother Henry on a clear June night around 1900, chipping for crystals at Macdui summit. Kellas watched a figure climb up from Lairig Ghru, wander around, and go back the same way. It was ten feet tall, the same height as Macdui's cairn. His brother saw no-one.

Another version of the same sighting (*Aberdeen Press & Journal* 1925) is recounted by W G Robinson who got it from the brother, Henry Kellas (who apparently did see something after all). In this account, they were on Macdui by daylight with some mist. The gigantic figure came towards them from the cairn. It passed into a dip, but before it could reappear they were running away down to Corrie Etchachan.

In the 1920s, early Scottish Nationalist Wendy Wood (*The Secret of Spey*) heard in Lairig Ghru an underground voice 'of gigantic resonance' speaking what appeared to be ancient Gaelic. Heavy footsteps, not in step with her own, followed her down to Whitewell. This happened before Collie's speech but was published in 1930. Though English, Wood had a Gaelic grandmother, so had at least some familiarity with the language. Her main climbing exploit was the removal of the lightning conductor from the statue of the Duke of Sutherland at Golspie.

In the early 1920s Tom Crowley, President of the Moray Mountaineering Club, was descending Braeriach (on the side of it *furthest* from Macdui). He heard footsteps behind and turned to see 'an undefined, misty figure with pointed ears, long legs, and feet with talons which appeared to be more like fingers than toes'. Crowley fled into Gleann Einich.

In May 1945 Peter Densham, a forester in Strathspey, felt on the summit of Macdui the presence of an unseen companion, then a cold hand on his neck, and heard a crunching noise behind him. He panicked, and found himself running uncontrollably towards Lurcher's Crag. At the last minute he managed to deflect his course away from the clifftops, but did not stop running until right past Loch Morlich 1,000 metres below. The story was transcribed by a representative of the Edinburgh Psychic College who interviewed Densham in 1949.

Richard Frere (climber of the V Diff classic Savage Slit in Coire an Lochain, 1945) recounted to Affleck Gray an experience of a friend camping at Macdui summit 'whose identity he was not at liberty to disclose'. A panic sensation was followed by a shadow crossing the moonlight that shone into his tent.

About 20yds away... a great brown creature was swaggering down the hill. He uses the word 'swaggering' because the creature had an air of insolent strength about it: and because it rolled slightly from side to side, taking huge measured steps. It looked as though it was covered with shortish, brown hair (yes, he asserts, most definitely brown), its head was disproportionately large, its neck very thick and powerful. By the extreme width of its shoulders compared to the relative slimness of its hips he concluded its sex to be male. No, it did not resemble an ape: its hairy arms, though long, were not unduly so, its carriage was extremely erect... He tells us that the creature was at least twenty feet in height. And he seeks to use elementary trigonometry to prove it.

The creature had passed behind an identifiable boulder, and its head was above the horizon. The unnamed friend used his ice axe to compute the monster presence at between 24 and 30 feet in height.

Syd Scroggie was alone at the Shelter Stone on a calm beautiful evening in 1942. Suddenly he saw a figure against the pale water of Loch Avon.

The loch glimmered behind his silhouette in the twilight, and I saw him pace slowly out of the blackness at one side of the water into the blackness at the other.

The figure wore a rucksack. Norwegian Commandos were training at Glenmore Lodge—that building is now Cairngorm Lodge Youth Hostel and preserves in the porch a bullet-hole inflicted by those rowdy Norwegians. As the figure didn't respond to his shouts, Scroggie concluded that it wasn't one of them, and so presumably a German agent parachuted in.

In October 1943 Alexander Tewnion was walking the hills alone for ten days, carrying a revolver to replenish supplies. In mist and with a storm approaching, he was heading down from Macdui summit towards Coire Etchachan when he heard loud footsteps behind.

A strange shape loomed up, receded, came charging at me! Without hesitation I whipped out the revolver and fired three times at the figure. When it still came on I turned and hared down the path, reaching Glen Derry in a time I have never bettered.

Not the most convincing but certainly the most entertaining experience happened to two Buddhists who were carrying their bikes through the Ghru in

1948. Captain Sir Hugh Rankin of Blairgowrie, a practising Mahayana (Tibetan) Buddhist, and Lady Rankin, a Zen Buddhist, met at the Pools of Dee a Presence.

He was between 6ft 3in and 6ft 4in. He was enormously broad—about 50 inches round the chest I should say. He had big limbs and big hands. He also had very big feet... His head was finely chiselled. His nose was neither aquiline nor Roman but was cast in the Indo-Aryan mould. He was olive in complexion. He had long flowing locks of medium dark hair. He was dressed in a long robe like people wear in the East, and had on sandals...

The Presence then addressed us—in Sanskrit I think... [but see Wendy Wood above: perhaps the language was actually Gaelic]. I replied in Urdu.

The Revd Countess of Mayo, herself a practising levitator, arranged an encounter with the 'Great White Brotherhood' of levitating interplanetary beings on Macdui for 1960. However, the publicity-shy Presences remained absent—this despite the encouragement of spiritual landing lights: eighteen world mountains, including Holdstock Down in Devon and Lurcher's Crag, having been specially charged up with cosmic energy. Dr King, founder and chairman of the Aetherius Society, did on a different occasion take part in a meeting of the Great White Brothers in their underground conference centre below the boulders of Ben Macdui.

Richard Webb, alone at the Shelter Stone after two days sheltering from storm, was hit by a feeling of terror so strong that he departed to cross Cairn Gorm with only two hours left of daylight, Garbh Uisge in spate, and winds strong enough to blow him over many times on the plateau.

But given the numbers of people now frequenting Ben Macdui, actual sightings since 1943 are rather few. There is just one recent encounter to suggest that the creature may have survived Alexander Tewnion's revolver shots…

Tom Robertson, 68, and Derek Blake, 32, camped on Macdui summit in 2004. Robertson told the *Daily Star*:

> *At about 1am after we climbed into our sleeping bags we heard the footsteps of something coming to the tent and heard mumbling noises outside. I looked up through the air vent in the roof and saw a large arm crashing down. The figure of what seemed like a yeti was standing over the tent, then all hell broke loose and it was trying to get in at us. I remember something landed on my foot. My*

*toes are black, kind of bruised. I have never been
so scared in all the 60 years I have been interested
in such things.*

*I don't know what it is but it wasn't human.
I reckon it could be the Grey Man or something
from outer space.*

He estimated the height of the yeti-type creature
at 12 feet, and attempted to photograph its two-foot
long footprints in the gravel. After a wet night in
the damaged tent they headed down at dawn, but
Robertson became exhausted and was eventually
carried out by the Cairngorm Mountain Rescue.

While some of the encounters just described happened
before 1925, they were disclosed and published
after Collie's story was already in circulation. More
intriguing are references to a grim presence before
Collie's after-dinner speech.

James Hogg (the Ettrick Shepherd), in his
second Highland Journey (about 1802) crossed Ben
Macdui, probably slept at the Shelter Stone, and
thought Loch Avon twenty miles long at least. In
a poem he describes an hoary sage who 'Beheld the
fahm glide o'er the fell'. This Fahm of Ben Macdui
is, according to the *Statistical Account of Scotland*
(Revd John Grant, 1790s)

somewhat larger than a mole, of a brownish colour, with a large head… in summer mornings it issues from its lurking places emitting a kind of glutinous matter fatal to horses if they happen to eat the grass.

But the spectre below is something else.

When lo! aloft on grey Cairngorm,
A form appeared that chilled his blood—
The giant Spirit of the Storm.
His face was like the spectre wan,
Slow gliding from the mystic isle;
His stature, on the nightly plain
Of smoke tower o'er the burning pile.

Red, red and grisly were his eyes;
His cap the moon-cloud's silver grey,
His staff the writhed snake, that lies
Pale, bending o'er the milky way.

… Beware the sprite of Avin-Glen!
James Hogg: Glen Avin (1813)

So what were the strange footfalls in the mist, the shadowy giant creature? The available answers are a

The Grey Man

natural being, a supernatural being, an illusion or mistake, and a hoax.

Some have suggested a large primate unknown to science, a relative of Bigfoot and the Yeti. One researcher (Loren Coleman, described as one of the world's leading cryptozoologists) even floats the idea of a late-surviving *Gigantopithecus*. Giganto lived on bamboo shoots; her extinction 800,000 years ago may even be down to competition from the giant panda. (So it's only fair do's that humans now extinguish the panda in return.) Gigantopithecus teeth were being sold as dragon bones in a Hong Kong pharmacy before the Second World War.

Bamboo does not grow on Ben Macdui; and neither does anything else much. So what does F Mor live on? Small beetles will not sustain a man, let alone a monster, and there are only so many ptarmigan eggs. For comparison, an eagle's feeding ground is twenty miles wide.

If he eats people, why doesn't he show as a trend in the mountain rescue statistics? We imagine him waiting for the clouds to come down so he can harvest the sandwich crusts around the cairn. In fact, it's only recently that the crusts have fallen thick enough for even a seagull or a crow to come up and eat them. While they're up there, the gulls and crows also eat the young ptarmigan—so, even if you don't mind feeding Fear Liath Mor, protect the ptarmigan by not scattering those sandwiches.

In that case, Ferlas Mor as a spirit of the supernatural? There's an epistemological difficulty. If there were verifiable evidence for any such creature, then the creature would be something from the natural world, thus contradicting its own supernature. Accordingly, physical evidence of Ferlas (as of the Deity Himself) is intrinsically impossible. Knowledge of the creature, if any, must be direct and personal, straight into the mind rather than out in the physical universe. Thus it or she may have been experienced directly by Prof Collie, but for the rest of us, there is only Collie's wild eye at the Cairngorm Club dinner. And when asked to believe something inherently non-existent, it must always be more rational to hypothesise a hoax or simple misapprehension, even on the part of a professor of Chemistry.

Brocken spectres
Be on Ben Macdui at dawn, on a day with foul weather clearing, or in winter above a cloud inversion—and you may be lucky enough to see a grey ghost striding across the vapours. As often as not, the shadowy figure will have a multicoloured rainbow halo all around him. (Or her, if you yourself happen to be female.) James Hogg saw it, as a young shepherd above the Ettrick vale, and was scared: but he stopped being scared once he'd worked out what it was. Namely, his own shadow thrown on the cloud surface by the low sun.

In two thirds of a lifetime of being on hills, I've seen it half a dozen times; once even on Arthur's Seat in the centre of Edinburgh—Hogg himself, or at least Robert Wringhim, the hero of his *Confessions of a Justified Sinner*, met one there as well: 'the little wee ghost of the rainbow'. The shape is the Brocken spectre, named after the high point of Germany's Harz Mountains. The rainbow halo is called the Glory, and the glory of it is that you see yourself and anyone beside you, but it's your own shadow that has the halo around its head.

Edward Whymper, descending the Matterhorn after his disastrous first ascent of it, was scared by what seems to have been a Brocken spectre, although the engraving he made later shows distortions in memory: the spectre is much larger than himself, and also above him.

What Alexander Kellas describes could be a spectre thrown not by sunlight but by the full moon. That would be a rare and most unsettling sighting, but the way the figure recedes and approaches is typical Brocken behaviour.

Brocken spectres are shadows, and shadows are silent. However, cavers are familiar with the way running water can be heard as human voices and footfalls. The Tailors' Burn and the March Burn both run across Ben Macdui's plateau within 500 metres of the summit. The human mind can also impose a regular footfall pattern into such random sounds as small avalanches.

However, the two large brown creatures could not be Brockens. The account by Richard Frere's unnamed friend contains one stark inconsistency:

by moonlight, however bright, the human eye can detect no colour—not even brown. Frere's friend's impression of brownness must have come out of his own brain; and I suspect the rest of the creature did as well, being an unusually exciting dream brought on by discomfort of his stony bed. The account from 2004 is admirably vivid—what a shame that Robertson, dedicated ghost-hunter, didn't have his camera set and ready beside his sleeping bag. What model of tent, though, allows such a clear view through the air vent? Mine has a minimal zip and no sightline at all.

But whether or not there was a physical creature on the mountainside, what did exist in Collie's consciousness was a sensation of panic. Pan, half god half goat, plays unsettling music on his reed pipe, and is the original sacred figurehead of the witches... and they think you can alleviate a panic attack using Prozac.

According to the UK National Health Service, one in ten of us will at some time suffer a panic attack, defined as at least four out of a list of fourteen symptoms (rapid, difficult breathing, sweating, wanting to run away very quickly, feelings of foreboding and death, pallor, chest pains, involuntary defecation, and so on). A panic attack is more likely when you're feeling anxious anyway—as when navigating in mist on Ben Macdui. John Buchan records one on the descent of the Alpspitze in the Bavarian Alps (2,682 metres, Wetterstein limestone with klettersteig chain-assisted scrambles). He was infected by his companion, a native Bavarian, who felt it first, and they both fled down the mountain. Buchan is an even more credible witness than Collie. Collie was only a professor of Chemistry: Buchan sat in the House of Lords and was governor-general of Canada.

The hoax hypothesis
It has been suggested that Collie was asked to speak at the dinner without forewarning and was annoyed. He is also said to have confessed, later, to having made the whole thing up. That would certainly be a plausible way to avoid having to tell the boring story yet again. Affleck Gray, author of a very thorough study of the Grey Man, convincingly dismisses the hoax hypothesis:

> *Those who knew the man intimately would instantly condemn this as a gross vilification of character. A study of his career and personality would probably convince the most ardent sceptic of Collie's utter sincerity, whether his story is judged to be the result of hallucination or otherwise.*

Collie's an interesting chap—does anyone else in the

world have all four of a Mountain, a Pinnacle, a Step and a Ledge named after him?—so I made that study of his career and personality anyway.

Did the professor of Chemistry have a sense of fun? His article 'The Oromaniacal Quest' describes an ascent of Ben Nevis in pastiche of an early alchemical text. Having just completed the first winter ascent of Tower Ridge, the climbers must descend the 'truly sopho-spagyric' steps into the Observatory then standing on the summit.

> *But beyond the portal a very thick miste and cimmerian darkness, an eclipsation, apprehended them, and the Three did stumble now this way and now that, so did they greatly fear even at this very end of their Quest, that beasts and creeping things of monstrous shape awaited them...*

Careful study of this piece does reveal it as being humorous in intent.

Collie wrote in more conventional style of his expedition to Nanga Parbat (1895, reaching 20,000 feet), and of climbs in the Alps and Caucasus. He also went exploring underneath Slieve League in western Ireland. By boat he penetrated below the mountain, into a cave haunted by mermaids and a large sea monster, not to mention the pink-and-green spotted sea pig.

The place was uncanny enough even without the spotted pig. Although the day was calm, resonating waves echoed between the cave walls, flickered the candle flame and tossed the boat about. 'Aha,' said Collie, 'here comes the great big beast, the serpent'— a remark which abruptly brought the expedition to an end.

Our boatmen were at once terrified, shouting to each other, pushing and half rowing the boat in a frenzy of fear. Amidst the bellowing noises of the various caverns leading out of the central hall, and the angry hisses of 'the beast, the serpent', we departed most hurriedly for the outer air.

So Collie has a previous record as a maker-up of mountain monsters. Having persuaded an Irish boatman, he may have been tempted to test whether educated Edinbourgeois could believe in the impossible after dinner. Buchan's panic attack would have been one source for his story: it was published, after all, in the SMC Journal. More subtly, the previous reference to 'Ferlie Mor' (cited above) was in the Cairngorm Club Journal for January 1921. Collie, the club's President, must have seen it there, and presumably also read Mr Baker's book, and relished the way these would offer to researchers an independent, pre-existing Macdui monster. He could even have picked up on the 'Sprite of Avin-Glen', as Hogg had been quoted in the SMC Journal in 1922.

On the other hand, let's not allow mere literary research to spoil a splendid legend. When asked in a poll by *Choices UK* in October 2005, 72 percent of Britons surveyed claimed a belief in God, and four percent (as also, it's said, Professor Collie himself) in the Loch Ness Monster. To believe, so far as possible, only in what actually exists—this is a minority taste. And it can't have survival value, or else us Loch Ness monster-loving humans would be extinct. We choose our beliefs to fit in with the social milieu, our stories because they connect with the ones already in our anthology. The proper discipline for analysing the Grey Man isn't biology, but literary criticism.

Notes and references

Affleck Gray: *The Big Grey Man of Ben Macdhui* (1978). Gray's reportage is not pernickety as to facts. For example, he says that James Hogg 'was acquainted with a man who "beheld the *fahm* glide o'er the fell"'. In fact Hogg poetically invented 'an hoary sage' who saw the fahm glide.

'Big Grey Man—the Evidence' by Jack Hastie (SMCJ 1998); a critical round-up of Gray's and some other evidence.

Unless otherwise stated, my references are re-quoted from Gray or Hastie.

(p153) Collie on Braeriach: 'A' Chuilionn', SMCJ Vol 4, reprinted in *Himalaya* (see below).

(p155) Wendy Wood: *The Secret of Spey* (1930) and biography in progress by Rowena A Love.

(p157) Scroggie: *Cairngorms Scene and Unseen* (SMC 1989) for the description. His German spy hypothesis is in Affleck Gray.

(p158) Tewnion: Gray cites *Scots Magazine* (June 1958).

(p159) King and Mayo: in Affleck Gray. This lacks only a witness called Prawn. For 'did' read 'says he did' or, strictly, 'Gray says he says he did'.

(p160) Webb: *The Angry Corrie* 38 (1998). Webb himself ascribes his attack to solitude and anxiety.

(p160) Robertson: an Internet page citing *Daily Star* 28 July 2004.

(p161) Hogg: *Noctes Ambrosianae* in Blackwood's Magazine.

(p163) Lauren Coleman: quoted in 'The Big Grey Man of Ben Macdhui & Other Mountain Panics' by Andy Roberts, *Fortean Review.*

(p168) John Buchan (Lord Tweedsmuir) describes his panic attack of 1911 in SMCJ 1942.

(p169) Collie 'The Oromaniacal Quest', SMCJ 1894, reprinted in *Himalaya* (below).

(p169) Collie underneath Slieve League: *Climbing on the Himalaya and Other Mountain Ranges,* published David Douglas, Edinburgh (1902).

ROUTE 17 *Lairig Ghru to Mhaim Col*

Start:	Linn of Dee
Distance to summit:	16km (10 miles)
Total ascent:	1,000m (3,300ft)

Follow Route 12 to cross the footbridge north of Derry Lodge. Turn left, along the north side of Luibeg Burn. After 2km fork down left to the bouldery ford of Luibeg Burn—or a footbridge 400 metres upstream. The path leads around the flank of Carn a' Mhaim and into Lairig Ghru. A branch path forks down left for footbridge to Corrour bothy, but keep ahead. Two kilometres later, fork up right on a small path that joins the Tailors' Burn (Allt Clach nan Taillear), follows it up quite steeply, then vanishes. Slant up right to reach a broad col at 800 metres altitude.

Ascend the flank of Ben Macdui on steep boulders with traces of path. At the plateau turn north-west across the top of the Tailors' Burn to the summit.

In descent: from the summit, head carefully south-east until you've found and crossed the Tailors' Burn—in mist it's easy to turn down towards Lairig Ghru too early.

How good? The easy route from Corrour, or for that matter from Cairn Toul, but otherwise a brutal combination of a very long walk in, followed by a long, steep, rough ascent.

17 The Big Fib

He has felt from his early youth all the privations to which he can be exposed in almost any circumstances of war. He has been accustomed to scanty fare, to rude and often wet clothing, to cold and damp houses, to sleep often in the open air or in the most uncomfortable beds, to cross dangerous rivers, to march a number of miles without stopping and with but little nourishment, and to be perpetually exposed to the attacks of a stormy atmosphere.

Does this sound like a hillwalker or mountaineer? Does this sound like you? It isn't you. Sir John Sinclair, in *Analysis of Statistical Account of Scotland* (1825), is describing the ancient and honourable Scottish profession of cattle-thief.

Up until 1745, suppose you wanted a long tiring trek through the hills with a chance of an interesting knife-fight along the way: you would gather like-minded companions, set off through the Lairig Ghru for the Angus Glens, and come back with some of their cattle. A hundred years later, in a profession almost as respectable and only slightly less adventurous, you could take the cows in the opposite direction towards the autumn markets at Crieff or Falkirk, or right down into England. And at ceilidhs and at the kirkyard gate, when they went 'and what do you do?' they'd understand what you were up to and give it some respect and possibly even want to have sex with you.

Today's walkers lack any such helpful explanation. The only people who get paid for getting wet on Ben Macdui are us writers—and even we don't get paid very much.

Real life is something we're stuck with. Walking up hills, however, is an optional add-on. Over 50 million of the UK's inhabitants find that they can manage without any mountains. Accordingly, those of us who put our feet to the granite have to make up some excuses. This business of walking up hills is based, at the very beginning, on one big lie. We walk up Ben Macdui; we walk back down again; and all the way up and all the way back down we're pretending we know why we're doing it.

For some of us, that pretended reason is the summit. The summit will usually be one of the harder places to get to; its altitude makes it intriguingly different from Edinburgh; it sometimes has a view. However, having taken as our task the hardest point on Ben Macdui, we then bend our endeavours to finding the least difficult way to get there. We spend time in guidebooks and money in shops, we hire a bike in Braemar, we try to be as clever as we can with maps. Once you accept that the task is the trig on Macdui, all the rest becomes rational. But as you stumble among the summit boulders, wet snow in your boot tops and down the neck of your jacket, a view of snowflakes at speed and the compass clutched in your fast-numbing hand, you may be wondering: is this actually fun?

At a fine restaurant, we don't aim for seven potatoes of 30mm and upwards in a single plateful. We mash the spuds childishly into the coulée of cranberries and eat them up, and never even ask ourselves what it's all about. Yet when we go up Ben Macdui, we pretend it's for a purpose. Like Syd Scroggie in Corrour Bothy 1955, we find it necessary to pull the woolly hat over our own eyes:

Down there in Dundee you live in a world crammed with insoluble problems, political, economic, industrial and sociological... What if we should devise a substitute problem now and again, not so easy that it can be simply solved, yet not so hard it does not permit of solution, granting we apply to it the maximum of mind, body and moral fibre of which we are capable; and so kidding ourselves, at least for a time... Each hill trip brings a catharsis to those who have the insight fully to perceive the horrors of the world. 'Och well,' I thought to myself as I pulled the woolly hat over my eyes, 'The hills are beautiful anyway, and maybe that's reason enough.' The experience was not one whit less valid, totally blind, than when I could see.

We need to pretend that our fun has a function. The model is taken, inappropriately, from the life of work. Here are 1,500 words of *Black Pig* to write before bedtime; here is a stadium to be ready by July. Here are eight bales of straw to be spun into pure gold by dawn tomorrow. And here are 284 hills to be topped off before you die.

'Just show us the way to the next Clach a' Bhlair,' as Lotte Lenya might have sung if Brecht had only been a bagger. 'Oh, don't ask why. Oh, don't ask why.' For given that you need a scheme, the 284 are a pretty good plan. They make a task that's big, but not impossibly big. They take you into most of the good bits of Scotland, and Scotland's most interesting weather conditions. They link together in threes and fours so as to get you onto that grand ridge of Carn a' Mhaim. The Skye ridge takes you onto real rock, and

Macdui makes you either a pretty fit person or else a mountain biker.

And as I've no wish myself to end up in front of the TV in that cardigan, I shan't argue with Lotte Lenya (who was, we may remember, Ms Rosa Klebb in the second James Bond film, and had poison poking from the toes of her boots...) No, we shan't ask why. The stories and the self-deception are necessary in these degenerate days, when, however often you trail down to the labour exchange, they never seem to need a cattle-thief.

Notes and references

New Spalding Club, *Historical Papers* 1895 p507, reports the Lairig Ghru as in use by cattle-thieves in the mid eighteenth century.

Syd Scroggie: *Cairngorms Scene and Unseen* (SMC 1989).

Index

If you have enjoyed this book, you may also be entertained by Ronald Turnbull's account of the life and times of Great Gable:

The Riddle of Sphinx Rock